THE ULTIMATE MUTUAL FUND GUIDE

19 Experts Pick the 33 Top Funds You Should Own

About the Author

Warren Boroson won the 1996 Journalism Award for Personal Financial Reporting given by American University and the Investment Company Institute Education Foundation. His articles have been published in *The New York Times Magazine, Reader's Digest, Family Circle, Woman's Day, TV Guide, Better Homes and Gardens*, and elsewhere. Among his 20 books are *The Ultimate Stock Picker's Guide* (Irwin), *Keys to Investing in Mutual Funds* (Barron's), *Mutual Fund Timing & Switching Strategies* (Probus), *How to Sell Your House in a Buyer's Market* (co-author; John Wiley & Sons) and *How to Buy a House with No (or Little) Money Down* (co-author; John Wiley & Sons).

A graduate of Columbia College, Mr. Boroson won the New Jersey Press Association's highest news-writing award in 1991. He teaches investment courses at Ramapo College in Mahwah, New Jersey, and at The New School in New York City. He also edits a newsletter, "Mutual Fund Digest."

Revised Edition

THE ULTIMATE MUTUAL FUND GUIDE

19 Experts Pick the 33 Top Funds You Should Own

WARREN BOROSON

Professional Publishing®
Chicago • London • Singapore

© Warren Boroson, 1993 and 1997

All rights reserved. No part of thes publication may be reproduced, stored in a retrieval system, or transmitted, in any form or by any means, electronic, mechanical, photocopying, recording, or otherwise, without the prior written permission of the publisher.

This publication is designed to provide accurate and authoritative information in regard to the subject matter covered. It is sole with the understanding that neither the author nor the publisher is engaged in rendering legal, accounting, or other professional service. If legal advice or other expert assistance is required, the services of a competent professional person should be sought.

From a Declaration of Principles jointly adopted by a Committee of the American Bar Association and a Committee of Publishers.

Times Mirror
Higher Education Group

Library of Congress Cataloging-in-Publication Data

Boroson, Warren.
   The ultimate mutual fund guide : 19 experts pick the 33 top funds you should own / Warren Boroson. — Rev. ed.
     p.   cm.
   Includes index.
   ISBN 0-7863-1130-4
   1. Mutual funds—United States.   2. Stockbrokers—United States--Interviews.   I. Title..
HG4930.B67   1997
332.63'27—dc20   96-43011

Printed in the United States of America
1 2 3 4 5 6 7 8 9 0 DO 3 2 1 0 9 8 7 6

PREFACE

This book is intended to be read by beginners as well as by sophisticated investors. Both groups should benefit from learning the answers that 19 mutual-fund authorities give to such gnarly questions as:

- How many stock mutual funds should an investor own?
- Which stock mutual funds should perform very profitably over the next two years?
- Which are the best and the worst mutual fund families? ("Best" means funds that bless you with more profit than you reasonably had a right to expect, given the funds' level of riskiness. A conservative fund gives you a very healthy profit; a risky fund gives you a stratospheric profit.)
- Might someone be well advised to own individual stocks as well as stock mutual funds? Individual bonds as well as fixed-income funds?
- When should an investor give up on a fund and sell the shares?
- Which kinds of funds should an investor own in a diversified portfilio, and which kinds should an investor ignore?
- What are the best ways to evaluate a fund's performance?

Also of interest to sophisticated investors, as well as beginners, will be the interviews with many of the most successful mutual fund managers (Chapters 25 through 41).

The first chapter is intended for beginners—and for sophisticated investors who wouldn't mind a review of the basics. Other sophisticated investors may choose to skip to Chapter 2.

Warren Boroson

AUTHOR'S NOTE

For their valuable help—with interviews, with the questionnaires, with transcriptions—I wish to thank Elaine Laramee, Linda H. Burgess, Peter Bridge, Jane Mahady, Aaron Elson, Vera Lawlor, Hali Helfgott, and Elise Young. I am also grateful to Morningstar, Inc., for generously providing data on the various funds.

W.B.

THE PANEL OF EXPERTS

Burton Berry
**No-Load Fund*X

Warren Boroson
Specialist Editor, The Record

Kurt Brouwer
Brouwer & Janachoski

William E. Donoghue
W.E. Donoghue & Co.

Professor William Droms
Georgetown University School of Business

Edward M. Higgins
Higgins Associates

Henrietta Humphries
Certified Financial Planner

Sheldon Jacobs
No-Load Fund Investor

Ram Kolluri
Individual Asset Planning Corp.

Craig Litman
Litman/Gregory & Company

Robert Markman
Markman Multifunds

Paul A. Merriman
Paul A. Merriman & Associates

Don Phillips
Morningstar, Inc.

Alan Pope (retired)
Sandia National Laboratories

Stephen Savage
The Value Line Mutual Fund Survey

Jay Schabacker
Schabacker Investment Management

Martin Skala
Independent Investment Consultant

John Stein, Ph.D.
Stein No-Load Mutual Fund Service

Ken Weber
Weber Asset Management, Inc.

CONTENTS

SECTION I

MUTUAL FUNDS: THE CHOICE FOR TODAY'S INVESTORS
1 A Brief Introduction to Mutual Funds 3
2 How to Use This Book 11
3 Understanding Fund Performance 15
4 The 19 Experts 23

SECTION II

THE EXPERTS' CHOICES
5 The 33 Best Funds 29
6 The 27 Runners-Up 61
7 The Single Best Fund 85
8 The Single Best, Overlooked Fund 89
9 Most Admired Portfolio Managers 101
10 The Best Families 107
11 The Worst Families 111
12 The Best Load Funds 115

SECTION III

ISSUES AND ANSWERS
13 Traders versus Investors 119
14 Open-Ends versus Closed-Ends 123
15 Six Ways of Evaluating Funds 127
16 Which Time Period to Stress? 133
17 The Worst Handicaps 137
18 Is Giant Size a Giant Handicap? 143
19 When to Sell 147
20 Why Some Funds Do Better Than Others 153
21 Why Some Managers Do Better Than Others 157
22 Assembling an Entire Portfolio 161
23 Just Funds—or Individual Securities, Too? 167
24 A Typology of Market-Timers 169

SECTION IV
INTERVIEWS WITH 17 TOP MANAGERS

25 Vanguard's John Bogle: "No Ifs, Ands, or Buts. Buy an Index Fund." 177
26 PBHG's Gary Pilgrim: "You Get Too Attached to These Companies." 181
27 Loomis-Sayles' Dan Fuss: "I Don't Even Have a Computer in My Office." 187
28 T. Rowe Price's Brian Rogers: "We're Willing to Take the Heat." 191
29 T. Rowe Price's Preston Athey: "It's Not a Glamorous Way to Invest." 195
30 Dodge & Cox's John A. Gunn: "Among Mutual Funds, We're a Strange Beast." 201
31 PIMCO's Bill Gross: "You Can Beat the House." 205
32 Twentieth Century's Glenn Fogle: "Comparing Other Funds with Giftrust Is Like Comparing Basketball Players to Michael Jordan." 207
33 T. Rowe Price's Chip Morris: "When the Death of the Computer Industry Is Announced, Double Up." 211
34 Janus' James P. Craig: "When You Get Stubborn, You Get into Trouble." 213
35 Janus 20's Thomas F. Marsico: "An Intuitive Nature Is a Big Plus." 219
36 Vanguard's Ian MacKinnon: "We Search Avidly for the Free Lunch." 223
37 The Yacktman Fund's Donald T. Yacktman: "I'm Eating My Own Cooking." 233
38 Mutual Series' Michael Price: "All This Nonsense That Wall Street Creates . . ." 235
39 Vanguard/Wellesley Income's Jack Ryan: "Most Income Investors Would Be Better Off Skipping the Highest-Yielding Stocks." 241
40 Fidelity Equity-Income II's Brian Posner: "I Try to Avoid Stocks That *Should* Be Cheap." 251
41 Oakmark's Robert J. Sanborn: "All in All, You Need Just Three Stock Funds." 257

APPENDIX: FOR MORE INFORMATION . . . 259
GLOSSARY 261
INDEX 269

SECTION I

MUTUAL FUNDS: THE CHOICE FOR TODAY'S INVESTORS

CHAPTER 1

A Brief Introduction to Mutual Funds

Most people begin to invest in mutual funds in their early 40s. By then, they have finally amassed enough spare money to invest; or perhaps they have learned the wisdom of putting their money into a portfolio of mutual funds as opposed to the folly of investing in a typical helter-skelter portfolio of individual stocks.

In fact, mutual funds in general can be regarded as a way of raising your chances of investing in stocks profitably instead of unprofitably. This new appreciation of mutual funds helps account for their growing popularity. Today, there are 6,000 different funds; in 1983, there were 1,025. Today, funds have $3 trillion in assets; in 1979, they had $94.5 million. In 1984, only 12.8% of all IRA money was in mutual funds; by the end of 1993, it was 32.7%—the largest for any financial product. Today about 15.6% of all household financial assets are invested in mutual funds—as opposed to only 2.0% in 1975. Back in 1979, mutual funds had nearly 10 million shareholders; in 1994 there were 89.6 million stock and bond accounts, representing 31% of all U.S. households.

In a short time, the Investment Company Institute reports, mutual funds have become the country's second largest financial institution, the assets exceeded only by those of commercial banks.

Since 1926, according to Ibbotson Associates in Chicago, large-company stock have returned 10.2% a year, with small-company stocks at 12.2%. Long-term government bonds have returned 5.4%, and intermediate-term government bonds have returned 5.1%. Cash equivalents—specifically, U.S. Treasury bills—have returned a mere 3.7%.

Of course, mutual funds also enable investors to put money into fixed-income investments (like corporate bonds), cash equivalents (like money-market funds), precious metals, options, and such. And without fixed-income mutual funds, investors might suffer the consequences of not having diversified portfolios. They also wouldn't have knowledgeable people making sure that the potential rewards of the fixed-income investments they buy match (or exceed) their riskiness—authorities who also ensure that the bonds' issuers don't start slipping down the tubes and the bonds' value begin disappearing.

But stocks are generally the riskier and potentially more rewarding investments, which is why the preeminent benefit of mutual funds is helping investors make money in the stock market.

A mutual fund is a company that buys securities for its investors—stocks, bonds, whatever. You buy, say, $1,000 worth of the shares of a mutual fund, and you will own a proportionate amount of all the securities that the fund has in its portfolio. (When you buy shares of a money-market mutual fund, you are buying shares of a company that concentrates on short-term debt. Money-market funds differ from funds in general in that [a] their price per share [net asset value] doesn't bob up and down—it's usually fixed at $1; and [b] money-market mutual funds never charge commissions.)

When people talk about "mutual funds," they usually mean "open-end" funds, where the investment company sells shares directly to the public and buys them back directly—rather than "closed-end funds," where investors buy and sell shares among themselves, on stock exchanges. This book focuses on the more popular open-end funds. (See Chapter 14 for a discussion of the pros and cons of closed-ends.) In 1991, investors in mutual funds were asked by the Investment Company Institute why they had chosen mutual funds over other financial products. Here are the responses:

Funds are more diversified.	60%
Funds have higher investment returns.	44%
Funds are more professionally managed.	43%
I prefer funds to picking my own investments.	31%
Funds are easier to invest in.	30%

The chief reason so many investors manage to lose money in the stock market may be that their holdings are not diversified. Their portfolios are skimpy, are concentrated in just a few areas, or both. They may own three or four stocks, or 12 stocks, but all of them utilities. Typical investors don't enjoy the safety in numbers. And just a few dogs can readily turn their houses into kennels.

What they should have, instead, is a substantial selection of stocks in different industries. (Fifteen stocks in nine industries is a common recommendation.) Which stocks you buy and when you should sell them can be important, of course, but not so important as diversity. You could just invest in a stock index fund—a mirror of a model of the stock market as a whole, like the Standard & Poor's 500 Stock Index—and do very nicely indeed.

Actually, investing in funds is a breeze. Obtain an 800 number for a particular fund (try the 800 directory: 800-555-1212). Phone and ask for a prospectus and an application; fill out the application (ask to have your distributions—interest, dividends, capital gains—reinvested); and send it in, along with a check for at least the minimum required for the first investment, which typically is $100 to $3,000.

The hard part, of course, is deciding which funds to buy. Mutual funds are a fairly recent product; in this country, they date back only to the 1920s. And it is startling how little agreement there is about the very basics of mutual funds.

Even the way mutual funds should be classified is in dispute. Yet investors need to know what they are buying: A portfolio of low-grade bonds? Small-company stocks? Gold stocks?

Knowing into what category a fund falls also helps you compare its performance with those of similar funds.

The simplified classification guides (Table 1–1 and Table 1–2), which are followed throughout this book, have been adapted from the classifications of Morningstar, Inc. (Definitions are provided in Chapter 3.)

TABLE 1-1

Classification of Stock Funds

Aggressive	Equity income
Small company	Specialty
Growth	Balanced
Growth and income	Asset allocation
International/Global	

TABLE 1-2

Classification of Bond Funds

Corporate	Global
Government	Municipal
International	

If you're going to create a portfolio of mutual funds for yourself, don't just buy funds according to their general classifications (growth, equity income, etc.), which are pretty crude. A more precise guide focuses on the kinds of investments a fund buys. If it's a stock fund, does it buy big-company stocks, mid-sized company stocks, or small-company stocks? Does it buy growth stocks (those of companies whose earnings keep climbing), value stocks (seemingly undervalued stocks), or a blend of growth and value stocks?

The "style boxes" in Table 1-3 will help you in creating a diversified portfolio.

Your fund portfolio should probably be all over the map. Large-company stocks tend to be out of step with small-company stocks, and the same is true of growth versus value stocks. And in general, it's nice to have a fairly stable portfolio—just in case you unexpectedly need money, or you panic and decide to sell everything in a bear market.

TABLE 1-3

Equity Style Box

	Investment Style	
Value	**Blend**	**Growth**
Large-cap value	Large-cap blend	Large-cap growth
Mid-cap value	Mid-cap blend	Mid-cap growth
Small-cap value	Small-cap blend	Small-cap growth

Even so, the more conservative you are, the more your portfolio should tilt toward the Northwest (large-company, undervalued stocks); the more adventuresome you are, the more your portfolio should tilt toward the Southeast (small, growth stocks). Large-company, undervalued stocks tend to be less volatile.

While value stocks seem to have performed better over the years than growth stocks, growth funds seem to have decisively beaten value funds—perhaps, as Morningstar has suggested, because there simply aren't many value funds buying small-company stocks. That's an argument for the daring investor to tilt toward growth funds—along with small-company value funds.

As for bonds, here the two dimensions aren't size of company and investment strategy, but maturity and credit quality. And here again, a diversified portfolio would be all over the place, but conservative investors might tilt toward the Northwest (short maturities, high quality), while aggressive investors might be drawn toward the Southeast (long maturities, low quality).

What else does a beginner need to know? Primarily that you should create an investment portfolio suitable to:

1. Your age and—if you are investing for them as well—the ages of your family members,
2. Your need for income,

3. Your investment sophistication or risk tolerance, and
4. Your goals (Retirement? Buying a house? Starting a business?).

Here is a conservative asset-allocation model that consists of just stocks, bonds, and cash. It was prepared by the American Association of Individual Investors in Chicago. The allocations depend on the investor's proximity to retirement and conservatism or aggressiveness.

	Stocks	Bonds	Cash
Five or More Years from Retirement:			
Conservative	40%	30%	30%
Aggressive	60%	30%	10%
Close to Retirement:			
Conservative	20%	50%	30%
Aggressive	40%	40%	20%
At Retirement:			
Conservative	0%	50%	50%
Aggressive	20%	50%	30%

A far more aggressive asset-allocation model suggests that you take your age, multiply it by 80% and put the *result* into the bonds—the *remainder* into stocks. Here's how it would work out at different ages:

Age	Stocks	Bonds
20	84%	16%
30	68%	32%
50	60%	40%
60	52%	48%
70	44%	56%

Notice that the older AAII asset-allocation model suggests that an aggressive investor, at retirement, have a mere 20% in stocks, whereas this newer model suggests that anyone age 70 have 44% in stocks. Thanks to the solid performance of the stock market in recent years, asset-allocation models have become more agressive.

Finally, invest in your portfolio gradually and regularly, not all at once. Use dollar-cost averaging, as it's called, so you don't put an enormous hunk of your worldly wealth into the stock market on a day like October 19, 1987, when the Dow-Jones Industrial Average lost 20% of its value. The remainder of this book will deal with such difficult questions as:

Which funds should you buy—and why?

Which are the best families of funds—and the worst?

How many funds should you own?

What different types of funds belong in a well-rounded portfolio?

When should you sell a fund?

CHAPTER

How to Use This Book

For this book, 18 mutual fund authorities—19 if one generously includes the author—answered such basic investing questions as: How many funds should be in your portfolio? Should you own individual stocks and bonds along with funds? Which funds would you think someone should actually buy for the next two years?

The authorities differed sharply on a number of matters, but there was rough agreement on the following:

- Apparently, the very best mutual funds are PBHG Growth, Mutual Discovery, Oakmark, Mutual Shares/Beacon, T. Rowe Price Equity-Income, Janus Overseas, Lindner Dividend, Northeast Investors Trust, Strong Government Securities, Vanguard Municipal Intermediate, and T. Rowe Price International Bond. These funds received the most nominations as best in their categories. (For the names of the 33 funds named most frequently, see Chapter 5.) These are funds suitable for anyone building or modifying an investment portfolio.
- If you already own shares of funds in the various categories listed in Chapter 5 (the winners) and are looking

for more diversity, scan the list in Chapter 6, which consists of the 27 runners-up.
- The most admired families are Vanguard, Fidelity, T. Rowe Price, and Mutual Series; see Chapter 10.
- Five to eight funds seem all that you need, according to the experts. For the categories you should consider in building a portfolio, see Chapter 22.
- Two good reasons to sell a fund: It changes its general strategy without a clear reason; and its performance has faltered badly and you cannot determine why. See Chapter 19.
- For a model portfolio, consisting of a variety of top funds, see Chapter 22.
- Should you buy individual stocks and bonds as well as mutual funds? Most panelists were skeptical of investors' buying individual stocks, but they inclined to be tolerant of their buying bonds. See Chapter 23.

The opportunity to pick the brains of 19 experts was not squandered, and they were asked a variety of fundamental questions about mutual funds, along with some questions thrown in just for fun.

- Which single conservative fund would they recommend—a fund that they would expect to do well over the next two years? (See Chapter 7.)
- Which excellent fund is the most overlooked? (Chapter 8)
- Which mutual fund manager do they admire most? (Chapter 9)
- Which families do they admire the least? (Chapter 11)
- Which are the best load funds? (Chapter 12)
- Do they prefer open-end funds, closed-end funds, or consider them equal? (Chapter 14)
- What are the best ways of evaluating a fund's record? (Chapter 15)
- In evaluating a fund, which time periods would they emphasize? (Chapter 16)

- What are the worst handicaps that funds may suffer from? (Chapter 17)
- Is giant size really a serious handicap? (Chapter 18)
- Why do some funds do better than others? (Chapter 20)
- Why do some managers do better than others? (Chapter 21)
- Do they practice any form of market-timing? (Chapter 24)

The chief disagreement among the panelists was over whether investors should be patient—giving funds plenty of time to prove themselves, even if they stumble along the way; or whether investors should be opportunistic—quickly selling whatever funds disappoint and moving on to fresh fields.

Investors might decide which camp they themselves prefer. Or they might consider emulating Alan Pope, an expert who separates his portfolio of funds into two categories: funds for investing and funds for trading. See Chapter 13.

This book also provides data on the 33 top-rated funds—everything from their 800 numbers (if they have one) to their standard deviations and minimum first investments. (Chapter 3 explains standard deviations, alphas, betas, and so forth.)

Then there are the 27 also-rans.

Before actually investing in any funds, an investor would be wise to learn something about the managers themselves—how they themselves describe their investment strategies, how they explain their successes, even what advice they would give people who invest in mutual funds. At the end of the book are interviews with portfolio managers whose funds made the top 33 or 27.

CHAPTER 3

Understanding Fund Performance

Essential data on the 33 top-rated funds are provided in Chapter 5. What follows is an explanation of that data. Here is a typical listing for a fund mentioned in this book, followed by a number corresponding to the explanation below:

1. Robertson Stephens Emerging Growth (small company)
2. Started: 1987
3. States available: All except AK, MD, OH, OR, SC, and WI
4. Description: Seeks capital appreciation . . .
5. Adviser: Robertson Stevens Investment Management
6. Address and phone: 555 California Street, Suite 2800, San Francisco, CA 94104; 415-781-9700; 800-766-FUND
7. Portfolio manager: Robert C. Czepiel, 1987
8. Standard deviation: 17.08
9. Beta: 1.03
10. Alpha: –2.4
11. R squared: 24
12. Minimum: $5,000
13. Minimum reinvestment: $100

14. Sales charges: 0.25% 12b-1 fee
15. Expense ratio: 1.56%
16. Turnover: 280%
17. Assets: $173.3 million
18. Annualized total return: 17.4%, 1 year; 18.04%, 3 years; 11.57%, 5 years.

1. The name of the fund and its Morningstar classification. Funds may be classified in different ways, depending on who is doing the classifying. Here are definitions of various classifications of stock mutual funds:

Aggressive growth fund: A fund that seeks maximum capital gains. It usually remains fully invested in stocks at all times; it buys small, speculative companies and depressed stocks; and it may employ techniques like selling short and using leverage. Aggressive growth funds tend to be especially volatile.

Small company: A fund that concentrates on small companies—though funds tend to define "small" differently.

Growth: A fund that invests in companies whose earnings are growing and that seem to have bright futures.

Growth and income: A combination growth fund and equity-income fund.

International/Global Stock: A fund that invests in the securities of foreign corporations.

Equity income: A fund that concentrates on blue chip stocks with high yields.

Specialty: Funds that specialize in a sector, like utilities, technology, and health.

Balanced: A fund that invests in both stocks and bonds—typically 60% in bonds, 40% in stocks.

Asset allocation: A fund that either keeps a fixed percentage of its assets in various instruments—bonds, stocks, precious-metals stocks, real-estate stocks—or varies the percentages, depending on where the fund managers think the investment markets are heading. A true asset-allocation fund has some investments in inflation-resistant hard assets (precious metals, real estate).

CHAPTER 3 Understanding Fund Performance   17

   2. One reason that the year in which a fund was launched is important: If it's a new fund, some investors would stay away, in view of the fact that the fund has only a short track record; other investors would be especially interested, figuring that the fund is still small and therefore relatively nimble in its investing tactics.
   3. If a fund doesn't sell its shares in your state, you might write to the fund's officers, to indicate that there are interested investors in your area. The fund's officers may wrongly believe that the cost of obtaining the state's permission outweighs any possible increase in shareholder purchases.
   4. The fund's description here comes from its prospectus.
   5. Most funds appoint advisers to manage the assets. Sometimes the adviser is not affiliated with the fund itself. Many funds in the Vanguard Group in Valley Forge, PA, for example, are managed by Wellington Advisors in Boston.
   6. An investor residing in the same state as a fund may not be able to use the fund's free 800 number. A few funds don't have 800 numbers for outsiders, Lindner being an example. (It's a penny-pinching fund.)
   7. Some investors are dubious of a fund with a good long-term record if the manager is new and isn't responsible for the superior long-term record.
   8. and 9. The standard deviation is a measure of the volatility of an investment, reflecting (in this case) how much a fund's price has bobbed up and down compared with its average price.
   Another measure of the volatility of an investment is its beta, which compares a fund's volatility with the volatility of Standard & Poor's 500 Stock Index or the Lehman Brothers Corporate/Government Bond Index.
   In general, the standard deviation is a better measure, one reason being that the movement of the prices of foreign stocks and gold doesn't correlate with the S&P 500's volatility.
   Here are typical betas of the average fund in a category:

	Beta
Stock	
Aggressive	1.00
Small company	0.85
Growth	0.95
Growth and income	0.90

International/Global Stock	0.81
Equity income	0.78
Specialty (varied)	0.92
Balanced	0.66
Asset allocation	0.60
Fixed-Income	
Corporate (general)	0.93
Government (general)	0.85
International/Global Bond	0.78
Municipal (national)	0.95

10. Investments are expected to reward you in line with their volatility. A volatile mutual fund, for example, should bless you with far greater profit than a stable fund. The "alpha" correlates a fund's volatility with the profits it gave its investors. An alpha of 0 (zero) means that the fund's performance was just as expected, given its beta. Any alpha above zero indicates that the fund has done better than expected; any alpha below zero indicates that a fund has done worse than expected.

But alphas can be crude measures of performance, and some funds among the top 33 have negative alphas.

11. R squared measures how faithfully a fund follows its index—typically, either the S&P 500 or the Lehman Brothers Bond Index. A loyal follower has an R squared of 100. A faithless follower has an R squared below zero. The number thus normally tells you two things:

A. How well diversified a fund is. Low numbers may mean a fund is not well diversified. High numbers may mean that it is well diversified.

B. How sensible it is to compare a fund with its index. International funds, obviously, don't correlate well with the S&P 500. That's why calculating their betas and alphas isn't very meaningful. Obviously, funds that invest in foreign bonds won't track the Lehman Brothers index.

12. and **13.** The minimum first investment may be lower for a tax-sheltered contribution, like an IRA. You may also be able to

CHAPTER 3 Understanding Fund Performance

persuade a fund to accept a lower minimum if you want to space out your investment into a fund ("dollar-cost averaging").

14. These are the highest front-end sales charges; large investors may get discounts. A low load is up to 3%; a medium load is 3% to 6%; and a full load is 6% to 8.5%. A 12b-1 fee is for marketing expenses; some investors consider a fee over 0.25% of assets a year unacceptable.

15. Other things being equal, investors should choose funds with low expense ratios.

The expense ratio indicates how efficient a fund is in keeping its costs down. It's the percentage of fund assets actually spent each year on operating expenses, management fees, and 12b-1 fees. Not included among expenses are trading costs, along with initial and deferred sales charges and redemption fees. Vanguard funds generally have low expense ratios. New funds tend to have high ratios. The average U.S. stock fund has an expense ratio of 1.34%; the average taxable fixed-income fund has an expense ratio of 1.08%. Obviously, the numbers vary by fund classifications. Among specialty funds, utilities tend to have low expenses and low turnovers, while technology funds have high expenses and high turnovers.

Type of Fund	Expense Ratio	Turnover
Stock		
Aggressive	1.75%	130%
Small company	1.52	86
Growth	1.44	89
Growth and income	1.25	62
International/Global	2.01	72
Equity income	1.37	64
Specialty	1.87	148
Balanced	1.32	87
Asset allocation	1.35	100
Fixed-Income		
Corporate (general)	0.98	145
Government (general)	1.10	184
International/Global Bond	1.46	233
Municipal (national)	0.97	70

16. The turnover measures the annual rate of a fund's buying and selling activity. A low turnover ratio (20%–30%) suggests that the fund follows a buy-and-hold strategy; a high turnover (over 100%) suggests an opportunistic strategy.

To quote *Morningstar:* "Funds compute this figure by dividing the lesser of the dollar amount of purchases or sales (excluding all securities with maturities under one year) by the fund's average monthly assets. (By looking at the lesser of purchases or sales, one does not account for the buying and selling of securities forced on a fund by investments or redemptions. The lesser [number] gives a clearer picture of managerial decisions.). . .

"Higher turnover usually incurs greater brokerage costs. One should be careful, however, in interpreting the turnover ratio. A turnover ratio of 100% or more does not necessarily mean that all securities in the portfolio have been traded. A turnover of 100% may mean that 1% of the portfolio was traded 100 times over the year, or that 25% of the portfolio was traded four times, etc."

Surprisingly, the funds with the highest turnover are government funds, because they keep changing the maturities of their holdings—the chief way they can beat the indexes.

17. Assets. With a stock fund, large size has traditionally been considered a handicap. (But see Chapter 18.) With fixed-income funds, giant size is considered a benefit: Such funds have the clout to buy up the most attractive issues.

18. Annualized total returns. These are the compounded average annual returns. If a fund's five-year annualized return is 10% a year, the fund did not appreciate by 10% a year. It could have gone up 35% in one year, and down 15% in another year. Instead, the total return over five years was reached *as if* the fund had appreciated by 10% a year.

SECTION II

THE EXPERTS' CHOICES

CHAPTER 4

The 19 Experts

The mutual fund authorities who participated in our poll included academics, journalists, money managers, authors, and newsletter editors.

The authorities:

After earning a business administration degree from Stanford University in 1943 and serving in World War II as a B-17 pilot, **Burton Berry** pioneered the use of no-load mutual funds for money management. He opened DAL Investment Co. in 1969 as a Securities and Exchange Commission-registered investment adviser and launched his newsletter, ***NoLoad Fund*X*, in 1976. Berry's latest book, updated and reissued, is *Loaded Questions on No-Load Funds*.

Warren Boroson is a specialist editor with *The Record*, a newspaper in Hackensack, New Jersey, and the author of *Keys to Investing in Mutual Funds* (Barron's Educational Publishing, second edition) and *Mutual Funds Timing and Tactics & Strategies* (Probus Publishing). He was the mutual funds columnist for *Sylvia Porter's Personal Finance Magazine*. He teaches a course on investing in no-load mutual funds at The New School in New York City. He has launched a newsletter, *Boroson's Mutual Fund Digest*. Boroson was the recipient of the 1996

Journalism Award for Personal Financial Reporting given by the Investment Company Institute and American University (for newspapers under 200,000 in circulation).

Kurt Brouwer is president of Brouwer & Janachoski, a San Francisco-based investment advisory firm managing over $350 million. The firm uses no-load mutual funds as its sole investment vehicle. He is the author of *Kurt Brouwer's Guide to Mutual Funds* and has written for *Forbes*, *Barron's*, and other publications. Brouwer is a graduate of the University of San Francisco with a degree in economics.

William E. Donoghue is chairman of W.E. Donoghue & Co., where he manages about $200 million in client portfolios of mutual funds. Bill is known for his support of innovative investment services, including money funds, no-load mutual funds, discount brokerage no-transaction-fee mutual fund programs, variable universal life insurance, and international stock and bond funds. He founded *Donoghue's Money Fund Report*, *Donoghue's MoneyLetter*, and the *Cash Manager* newsletter. His investment guides, including *Complete Money Market Guide*, *No-Load Mutual Fund Guide*, and others, have a total of 1.2 million copies in print.

William G. Droms is professor of finance in the School of Business of Georgetown University, Washington, D.C. He is a Chartered Financial Analyst. Among the eight books he has written are *No-Load Mutual Funds* (with Peter Heerwagen) and *The Dow Jones-Irwin Mutual Fund Yearbook* (1984 and 1985). His proprietary asset-allocation system is used by Minnesota Mutual's MIMLIC mutual fund family.

Edward M. Higgins is president of Higgins Associates in Cambridge, Massachusetts, an investment firm that specializes in no-load mutual funds and other commingled vehicles. He has a B.A. from Tufts and an M.S. from Boston University. Among his company's clients are Tufts/New England Medical Center, Western Union Corporation, Addison-Wesley Publishing Company, and Connecticut Conference of Municipalities.

Henrietta Humphries is a Certified Financial Planner and registered investment adviser. She has a master's degree from Stanford University's Graduate School of Business and has over 20 years' experience working with individuals and businesses. The author of *Take Charge! A Step-by-Step Guide to Managing Your Money*, Ms. Humphries frequently speaks on such topics as mutual funds, the economic outlook, tax strategies, and the best investments for the current year.

USA Today calls **Sheldon Jacobs** "the dean of the no-load fund watchers." Jacobs wrote the first book on no-loads back in 1974. He is now the editor and publisher of *The No-Load Fund Investor*, *The Handbook for No-Load Fund Investors*, and *Sheldon Jacobs's Guide to Successful No-Load Fund Investing*. He is also president of The BJ Group, a registered investment advisory that manages over $200 million in no-load funds for clients.

Ram Kolluri, CFP, M.B.A., is the head of Individual Asset Planning Corp. in Princeton, New Jersey. He started his investment career in 1980 as a financial consultant with Merrill Lynch, and now he specializes in no-load mutual funds.

Craig Litman (J.D., M.B.A.) is a mutual fund specialist advising high net worth individuals. Before founding Litman/Gregory & Company in 1987, he was vice-president and senior financial consultant at the investment management firm of Bailard, Biehl & Kaiser. He was a practicing lawyer before entering the investment business in 1983. He is co-editor of the *No-Load Fund Analyst*.

Robert Markman is the manager of the Markman Multifunds in Minneapolis, as well as president of Markman Capital Management, a registered investment advisory firm with over $400 million under management. A 15-year veteran of the mutual fund industry, Markman has been called "one of the nation's shrewdest judges of no-load funds" by Louis Rukeyser's *Wall Street Week*.

Paul Merriman of Seattle edits the newsletter *Fund Exchange* and runs the Merriman family of funds, with $160 million under management. He is the author of *Investing for a Lifetime* and *Market-Timing with No-Load Mutual Funds*. "We are the nation's only full-service market-timing organization. And I am probably the only mutual fund manager actively recommending our competition. I will consult with individuals as to which mutual funds are most likely to meet their long-term needs, and I do not charge for that service."

Don Phillips is president of Morningstar, Inc. in Chicago, the mutual fund publishing company. He has a B.A. from the University of Texas and an M.A. from the University of Chicago. Don joined

Morningstar in 1986 as the firm's first mutual fund analyst. He worked subsequently as the editor of *Morningstar Mutual Funds* and as publisher of the firm's managed-products divisions. He was recently named to *Worth Magazine's* list of 50 most influential people in global finance.

Alan Pope, a retired scientist in Punta Gorda, Florida, is the author of *Financial Success for Salaried People, Modern Investing in No-Load Funds,* and *Successful Investing in No-Load Funds.* He has been a student of mutual funds for 40 years. "I think being a research scientist helps me evaluate data, and teaching a no-load fund course helps me be conservative."

Stephen Savage is the editor and executive director of *The Value Line Mutual Fund Survey,* one of the nation's leading sources for mutual fund ratings and analysis. He joined Value Line in March 1993 to run and develop its mutual fund information business. He began his career in 1981 at MPL Communications in New York as a research analyst covering mutual funds while pursuing his degree at New York's Hunter College. He became editor of the *American Money Report* in 1983 and in 1985 launched the *Blue Book of Mutual Fund Reports,* a loose-leaf service devoted to rating and analyzing mutual funds. In 1987, Savage joined Wiesenberger Investment Companies Service as editor. In 1991, he was instrumental in the merger between fund evaluation services CDA and Wiesenberger, which were owned but run independently by International Thomson. In 1993, Savage left CDA/Wiesenberger to join Value Line. Savage has written for such publications as *Barron's, Individual Investor,* and *Financial Planning* magazine.

Jay Schabacker is president of Schabacker Investment Management in Rockville, Maryland, and editor of *Mutual Fund Investing.* He has been in the investment business for over 30 years. An engineering graduate of Cornell University, he holds an M.B.A. in finance and investments from George Washington University.

Martin Skala is an independent investment consultant. He was formerly a business and financial reporter with the *Christian Science Monitor.* He has an M.A. in economics from Columbia University.

John Picard Stein, Ph.D., president of Stein No-Load Mutual Fund Service in Venice, California, manages $9 million in mutual fund portfolios. Formerly an academic economist, educated at Harvard and the University of Chicago, he has been managing portfolios of no-load mutual funds on a fee-only basis since 1981.

Ken Weber is president of Weber Asset Management, an investment advisory firm in Great Neck, New York. The firm manages more than $80 million, all in no-load or low-load mutual funds. For 10 years (1982–1992), he wrote and published *Weber's Fund Advisor,* a widely read mutual fund newsletter.

CHAPTER 5

The 33 Best Funds

Our panel of 19 authorities judged the 33 open-ended investment companies listed in this chapter as best mutual funds in their categories—the ones most likely to do well over the next few years.

The big winners, the very top vote-getters in their categories, were PBHG Growth, Mutual Discovery, Oakmark, Mutual Shares/Beacon (I combined them), T. Rowe Price Equity-Income, Janus Overseas, Lindner Dividend, Northeast Investors Trust, Strong Government Securities, Vanguard Municipal Intermediate, and T. Rowe Price International Bond—a murderers' row of mutual funds.

The single largest vote-getter was T. Rowe Price Equity-Income, with nine nominations. Impressive indeed, but our panelists split their votes between two keen rivals, Fidelity Equity-Income and Fidelity Equity-Income II. Together, the two Fidelity funds also received nine votes.

A few of the top 33 also made the list of 46 best funds three years ago. Lindner Dividend was the top vote-getter at that time, with 11 nominations. Oakmark was top aggressive/small cap fund then, with four votes. This time, it was the top vote-getter in the growth category, with eight votes. There were 13 other repeaters:

Vanguard/Wellesley Income, Mutual Shares/Beacon, Scudder Growth and Income, T. Rowe Price International, Fidelity Equity-Income II, T. Rowe Price Equity-Income, Vanguard Equity-Income, Invesco Strategic Health, Vanguard/Wellington, Vanguard GNMA, Strong Government, Vanguard Municipal Intermediate, and T. Rowe Price International Bond.

Spectacular debuts were made by Vanguard Index 500, which went from total obscurity last time to the top 33 with four votes, and Mutual Discovery, a new fund, which went from zero to seven votes.

In the previous poll, two rounds of questionnaires went to the panelists, and funds that fell by the wayside on the second poll were relegated to a list of 47 runners-up. This time there was only one poll, and funds receiving only two votes were relegated to the list of runners-up.

Funds that did exceptionally well in the previous poll, but were totally ignored this time, include Monetta, Scudder International Bond, and Gateway Index Plus, all of which have stumbled badly. (Scudder International lost its portfolio manager.)

The 33 funds are not, of course, the only very fine funds that someone can invest in. Other excellent choices might have been bypassed simply because the competition in their categories—equity-income, growth, etc.—was so fierce. Among the runners-up, for example, were such heavyweights as Brandywine, Kaufmann, Fidelity Low-Priced Stock, Janus, and SoGen International.

The panelists had been asked to nominate one to three funds in each category, so that the maximum number of votes a fund could receive was 19. T. Rowe Price Equity-Income, therefore, appeared on almost every other panelist's list—an impressive accomplishment.

Of the 33 top funds, the family with the most offspring honored was Vanguard, with eight votes. While this is no small accolade, Vanguard's advantage in fixed-income investments played a big role: Three of its most-nominated funds are in that category. (Vanguard's low expenses are legendary, and low expenses and high-ranking fixed-income funds go hand in hand.)

T. Rowe Price was in second place, with five nominations. This family has gotten better and better. Fidelity, the largest fund family, also acquitted itself with honor, garnering three nominations. Invesco and Strong each had two. Scudder went from four in the previous poll to one this time.

Listed below are the 33 top-scoring funds. The number after each name indicates how many nominations each received. The listing is followed by each fund's profile, with data supplied by Morningstar.

FUNDS RECOMMENDED MOST FREQUENTLY
Stock Funds

Aggressive Growth
1. PBHG Growth (8)
2. Fidelity Contrafund (3)
3. 20th Century Ultra (3)

Small Company
4. Mutual Discovery (7)
5. T. Rowe Price Small Cap Value (3)

Growth
6. Oakmark (8)

Growth and Income
7. Mutual Shares/Beacon (8)
8. Fidelity Growth and Income (4)
9. Vanguard Index 500 (4)
10. Scudder Growth and Income (3)

International/Global
11. Janus Overseas/Worldwide (5)
12. Warburg Pincus International Equity (4)
13. Hotchkis and Wiley (3)
14. T. Rowe Price International Stock (3)
15. GAM International (3)

Equity Income
16. T. Rowe Price Equity-Income (9)

17. Fidelity Equity-Income 2 (7)
18. Vanguard Equity-Income (5)

Specialty
19. Vanguard Special Health (4)
20. T. Rowe Price Science & Technology (4)
21. Invesco Strategic Health (3)

Balanced
22. Dodge & Cox Balanced (6)
23. Vanguard Wellington (6)
24. Invesco Balanced (3)

Income
25. Lindner Dividend (6)
26. Vanguard/Wellesley Income (5)

Fixed-Income Funds

Corporate Bond
27. Northeast Investors Trust (6)
28. Strong Corporate Bond (3)

Government Bond
29. Strong Government Securities (4)
30. Vanguard GNMA (3)

International/Global bond
31. T. Rowe Price International (5)

Municipal Bond
32. Vanguard Municipal Intermediate (4)
33. Vanguard Insured Long-Term (3)

CHAPTER 5 The 33 Best Funds

STOCK FUNDS

Aggressive Growth

PBHG Growth

Started: 1985

States available: All plus PR

Description: The fund normally invests at least 65% of its assets in common stocks and convertible securities issued by companies with market capitalizations or annual revenues not exceeding $1.5 billion. Managers seek companies with potential for significant earnings growth and capital appreciation. Up to 15% of the fund's assets may be invested in foreign securities. Up to 5% of its assets may be invested in warrants and rights.

Adviser: Pilgrim Baxter & Associates

Address and phone: 680 East Swedesford Road, Wayne, PA 19087-1658; 800-433-0051

Portfolio manager: Gary L. Pilgrim

Standard deviation: 18.86

Beta: 1.17

Alpha: 14.4

R squared: 25

Minimum: $2,500

Minimum reinvestment: None

Sales charges: None

Expense ratio: 1.50

Turnover: 119%

Assets: $2028.1 million

Annualized total returns: 32.16%, 3 years; 35.08%, 5 years; 22.80%, 10 years

Fidelity Contrafund

Started: 1967

States available: All

Description: In its quest for capital appreciation, the fund invests primarily in common stocks and convertible securities that appear undervalued. It also may invest in preferred stocks, warrants, and debt securities. The managers seek companies that are unpopular with investors, but have strong long-term outlooks. The fund may invest up to 5% of its assets in lower-quality debt obligations.

Adviser: Fidelity Management & Research

Address and phone: 82 Devonshire Street, Boston, MA, 02109; 800-544-8888

Portfolio manager: Will Danoff

Standard deviation: 9.91

Beta: 0.91

Alpha: 2.2

R squared: 58

Minimum: $2,500

Minimum reinvestment: $250

Sales charges: 3.00%

Expense ratio: 0.96

Turnover: 223%

Assets: $15753.4 million

Annualized total returns: 16.30%, 3 years; 21.57%; 5 years; 19.18%, 10 years

20th Century Ultra

Started: 1981

States available: All

Description: Seeks capital growth. The fund typically invests at least 90% of assets in equity securities selected for their potential to appreciate. Most of these securities are common stocks of companies that meet the fund's standard for earnings and revenue trends. The fund may purchase securities only of companies that have operated for at least three years.

Adviser: Investors Research

Address and phone: 4500 Main Street, P.O. Box 419200, Kansas City, MO 64141-6200; 800-345-2021; 816-531-5575

CHAPTER 5 The 33 Best Funds

Portfolio managers: James E. Stowers III, Christopher K. Boyd, Derek Felske
Standard deviation: 15.98
Beta: 1.17
Alpha: 0.9
R squared: 36
Minimum: $2500
Minimum reinvestment: $50
Sales charges: None
Expense ratio: 1.00
Turnover: 87%
Assets: $14551.2 million
Annualized total returns: 17.36%, 3 years; 25.00%, 5 years; 19.81%, 10 years

Small Company

Mutual Discovery

Started: 1993
States available: All plus PR, GU, VI
Description: Seeks long-term capital appreciation. The fund invests primarily in companies with small market capitalizations. Among its purchases are common and preferred stocks, convertibles, and bonds of any quality. The fund seeks securities that are undervalued based on book, cash flow, and earnings value. It may invest up to 50% of assets in companies undergoing large-scale transformation, such as merging or reorganizing. Up to 50% of the fund's assets may be in foreign issues.
Adviser: Heine Securities
Address and phone: 51 John F. Kennedy Parkway, Short Hills, NJ 07078; 800-553-3014; 201-912-2100
Portfolio manager: Michael F. Price
Standard deviation: 7.97
Beta: 0.68

Alpha: 8.0
R squared: 49
Minimum: $1000
Minimum reinvestment: $50
Sales charges: None
Expense ratio: N.A.
Turnover: N.A.
Assets: $1559.4 million
Annualized total returns: 31.15%, 1 year; 21.17%, 3 years, 22.92%, inception

T. Rowe Price Small Cap Value

Started: 1988

States available: All plus PR

Description: Seeks long-term capital growth. The fund invests primarily in small companies using a value-oriented approach. Undervalued securities are identified by examining assets, earnings, cash flow, and franchises. Up to 20% of the fund's investments may be in foreign issues. Five percent of its assets may be invested in debt. When it was known as PEMCO (prior to June 30, 1988), the fund was open only to partners of Peat, Marwick, & Mitchell.

Adviser: T. Rowe Price Associates

Address and phone: 100 East Pratt Street, Baltimore, MD 21202; 800-638-5660; 410-547-2308

Portfolio manager: Preston Athey

Standard deviation: 7.19

Beta: 0.58

Alpha: 5.3

R squared: 42

Minimum: $2,500

Minimum reinvestment: $100

Sales charges: None

Expense ratio: 0.98

Turnover: 18%

Assets: $869.7 million
Annualized total returns: 16.28%, 3 years; 20.59%; 5 years; 13.39%, inception

Growth

Oakmark

Started: 1991
States available: All
Description: Seeks long-term capital appreciation with income among the manager's considerations. The fund invests largely in common stocks and convertibles. In determining value, the fund analyzes a company's ability to generate cash. It also considers the quality of management and the number of shares owned by management. The fund focuses especially on securities that are priced lower than their long-term value. The fund may invest up to 25% of its assets in foreign issues or debt securities. Up to 5% may be invested in emerging markets.
Adviser: Harris Associates
Address and phone: 2 North LaSalle Street, Chicago, IL 60602-3790; 800-625-6275
Portfolio manager: Robert J. Sanborn
Standard deviation: 8.96
Beta: 0.88
Alpha: 6.4
R squared: 65
Minium: $2,500
Minimum reinvestment: $100
Sales charges: None
Expense ratio: 1.17
Turnover: 18%
Assets: $3637.3 million
Annualized total returns: 36.30%, 1 year; 21.92%, 3 years; 33.06%, inception

Growth and Income

Mutual Shares/Beacon

Started: 1961

States available: All plus PR, GU, VI

Description: Income is secondary to capital appreciation. The fund's assets include common and preferred stocks and corporate debt securities of any credit quality. These securities are trading below their intrinsic value, according to price/book ratio, price/earnings ratio, and cash flow. Up to 50% of its assets may be invested in companies undergoing tremendous change. The fund also invests in foreign securities and securities of other investment companies.

Adviser: Heine Associates

Address and phone: 51 John F. Kennedy Parkway, Short Hills, NJ 07078; 900-553-3014; 201-912-2100

Portfolio manager: Michael F. Price

Standard deviation: 6.79

Beta: 0.67

Alpha: 5.5

R squared: 66

Minimum: $5,000

Minimum reinvestment: $100

Sales charges: None

Expense ratio: 0.69 (shares)

Turnover: 79% (shares)

Assets: $4007.2 million

Annualized total returns: 18.17%, 3 years; 18.21%, 5 years; 15.90%, 10 years

Fidelity Growth and Income

Started: 1985

States available: All

Description: Seeks long-term growth, current income, and growth of income. The fund invests largely in dividend-paying common stocks with growth potential.

Managers generally sell securities whose dividends fall below the yield of the S&P 500 Index. But some common stock picks may be in securities offering prospects for capital growth or future income instead of dividends. Fixed-income investments are usually based on corporate bonds.

Adviser: Fidelity Management & Research

Address and phone: 82 Devonshire Street, Boston, MA 02109; 800-544-8888

Portfolio manager: Steven Kaye

Standard deviation: 7.71

Beta: 0.86

Alpha: 3.6

R squared: 85

Minimum: $2,500

Minimum reinvestment: $250

Sales charges: None

Expense ratio: 0.77

Turnover: 67%

Assets: $16905.9 million

Annualized total returns: 18.48%, 3 years; 18.24%, 5 years; 17.48%, 10 years

Vanguard Index 500

Started: 1976

States available: All plus PR, GU, VI

Description: Seeks results that correspond with the performance of the S&P 500 Index. The fund allocates the percentage of net assets each company receives on the basis of the stock's relative total-market value: its market price per share times the shares outstanding. Prior to December 21, 1987, the fund name was Vanguard Index Trust. Prior to 1980, it was First Index Investment Trust.

Adviser: Vanguard's ore Management Group

**Address and phor   iguard Financial Center, P.O. Box 2600, Valley Fo   482; 800-662-7447; 610-669-1000

Portfolio manager: George U. Sauter
Standard deviation: 8.31
Beta: 1.00
Alpha: -0.1
R squared: 100
Minimum: $3,000
Minimum reinvestment: $100
Sales charges: None
Expense ratio: 0.20
Turnover: 4%
Assets: $19791.0 million
Annualized total returns: 15.99%, 3 years; 14.82%, 5 years; 14.18%, 10 years

Scudder Growth and Income

Started: 1984
States available: All
Description: Seeks growth of capital, current income, and growth of income. Managers invest primarily in common stocks that pay dividends, preferred stocks, and convertible securities. It may buy nondividend-paying common stocks and bonds. The fund may invest in foreign securities. In 1992, the fund absorbed about $215 million in assets of closed-end Niagara Shares. In 1991, Scudder Equity-Income Fund merged into this fund. Before November 13, 1984, the fund was named Scudder Common Stock Fund.
Adviser: Scudder Stevens & Clark
Address and phone: 2 International Place, Boston, MA 02110; 800-225-2470; 617-439-4640
Portfolio managers: Robert T. Hoffman, Benjamin W. Thorndike, Kathleen T. Millard
Standard deviation: 8.47
Beta: 0.93
Alpha: 1.6
R squared: 83

Minimum: $1,000
Minimum reinvestment: $100
Sales charges: None
Expense ratio: N.A.
Turnover: N.A.
Assets: $3537.6 million
Annualized total returns: 17.11%, 3 years; 15.79%, 5 years; 13.38%, 10 years

International/Global

Janus Worldwide

Started: 1991
States available: All plus PR, GU, VI
Description: Seeks long-term growth of capital consistent with preservation of capital. Nearly all of its assets are in foreign and domestic common stocks. Its portfolio is usually spread across at least five countries. Common stock investments are chosen from companies that are seeing demand for their products or services. The fund may engage in futures and options strategies.
Adviser: Janus Capital
Address and phone: 100 Fillmore Street, Suite 300, Denver, CO 80206-4923; 800-525-8983
Portfolio manager: Helen Young Hayes
Standard deviation: 10.54
Beta: 0.89
Alpha: 3.6
R squared: 45
Minimum: $1,000
Minimum reinvestment: $50
Sales charges: None
Expense ratio: 1.23
Turnover: 142%
Assets: $1805.0 million

Annualized total returns: 8.89%, 1 year; 17.19%, 3 years; 17.29%, inception

Warburg Pincus International Equity-Common Shares

Started: 1989

States available: All plus PR

Description: The fund seeks capital appreciation. It normally invests at least 65% of its assets in common stocks issued in at least three countries. The fund may from time to time invest a significant portion of its assets in one country, usually Japan.

Adviser: Warburg Pincus Counsellors

Address and phone: 466 Lexington Ave., New York, NY 10017-3147; 800-257-5614

Portfolio manager: Richard H. King

Standard deviation: 15.46

Beta: 0.86

Alpha: 5.7

R squared: 20

Minimum: $2,500

Minimum reinvestment: $100

Sales charges: None

Expense ratio: 1.44

Turnover: 17%

Assets: $2072 million

Annualized total returns: 26.68%, 1 year; 18.06%, 3 years; 12.14%, 5 years

Hotchkis and Wiley International

Started: 1990

States available: All

Description: Seeks current income and long-term growth of income and capital. Managers invest in equity securities of at least three non-U.S. markets. When considering companies, the fund seeks low price-earnings multiples, high dividend yields, high cash flow, and a low ratio of market price to book value. Convertible securities in the portfolio must carry a rating of at least A, or be of comparable quality. Before October 7, 1994, the fund was Olympic Trust International Fund.

Adviser: Hotchkis & Wiley

Address and phone: 800 West Sixth Street, Fifth Floor, Los Angeles, CA 90017; 800-346-7301; 213-362-8900

Portfolio manager: Sarah H. Ketterer

Standard deviation: 12.03

Beta: 0.81

Alpha: 5.4

R squared: 29

Minimum: $5,000

Minimum reinvestment: None

Sales charges: None

Expense ratio: 1.00

Turnover: 24%

Assets: $77.0 million

Annualized total returns: 18.07%, 3 years; 13.71%, 5 years

T. Rowe Price International Stock

Started: 1980

States available: All plus PR

Description: Seeks total return on assets from long-term growth of capital and income. The fund primarily invests at least 65% of its assets in the common stocks of established foreign issuers. The remainder may be in preferred stocks, warrants, convertible securities, and/or debt securities. Investments are usually maintained in at least three foreign countries. The fund may invest in both industrialized and developing countries. Prior to September 10, 1986, the fund was named T. Rowe Price International Fund.

Adviser: T. Rowe Price Investment Services

Address and phone: 100 East Pratt Street, Baltimore, MD 21202; 800-638-5660; 410-547-2308

Portfolio manager: Martin G. Wade

Standard deviation: 12.70
Beta: 0.81
Alpha: 2.3
R squared: 26
Minimum: $2,500
Minimum reinvestment: $100
Sales charges: None
Expense ratio: 0.91
Turnover: 18%
Assets: $6491.5 million
Annualized total returns: 14.63%, 3 years; 9.87%, 5 years; 15.51%, 10 years

GAM International

Started: 1985
States available: All plus PR
Description: Seeks long-term capital appreciation by normally investing at least 65% of its assets in securities issued in at least three foreign countries. Its primary focus is on equity securities, though it may have a substantial portion of its assets in debt securities. No more than 5% of its assets may be invested in debt securities below investment grade. The fund may purchase American and European depositary receipts.
Adviser: GAM International Management
Address and phone: 135 East 57th Street, 25th Floor, New York, NY 10022; 800-426-4685; 212-407-4600
Portfolio manager: John R. Horseman
Standard deviation: 16.22
Beta: 0.57
Alpha: 14.8
R squared: 8
Minimum: $1,000
Minimum reinvestment: $1,000
Sales charges: 5.00%

Expense ratio: N.A.
Turnover: N.A.
Assets: $450.7 million
Annualized total returns: 22.78%, 3 years; 16.76%, 5 years; 19.57%, 10 years

Equity-Income

T. Rowe Price Equity-Income

Started: 1985
States available: All plus PR
Description: Goals are dividend income paired with potential for capital appreciation. At least 65% of the assets are in income-producing common stocks. When examining securities, the fund reviews the yield and prospects for earnings and dividend growth, the relative valuation, and the competitive and financial strength of the company. On February 7, 1992, Bell Atlantic Equity Portfolio merged with this fund.
Adviser: T. Rowe Price Associates
Address and phone: 100 East Pratt Street, Baltimore, MD 21202; 800-638-5660; 410-547-2308
Portfolio manager: Brian C. Rogers
Standard deviation: 6.58
Beta: 0.75
Alpha: 4.0
R squared: 89
Minimum: $2,500
Minimum reinvestment: $100
Sales charges: None
Expense ratio: 0.96
Turnover: 46%
Assets: $5214.8 million
Annualized total returns: 16.98%, 3 years; 18.01%, 5 years; 15.06%, 10 years

Fidelity Equity-Income II

Started: 1990

States available: All

Description: Primary focus is income. Potential for capital appreciation is also considered. At least 65% of the fund's assets are in income-producing equity securities. Fund managers seek a yield that exceeds the composite yield of the S&P 500 Index. Other assets may be in debt securities of any type or credit quality. The fund may invest in foreign securities, enter into currency-exchange contracts, and invest in stock-index futures and options.

Adviser: Fidelity Management & Research

Address and phone: 82 Devonshire Street, Boston, MA 02109; 800-544-8888

Portfolio manager: Brian S. Posner

Standard deviation: 7.98

Beta: 0.85

Alpha: 2.0

R squared: 75

Minimum: $2,500

Minimum reinvestment: $250

Sales charges: None

Expense ratio: 0.75

Turnover: 45%

Assets: $11977.0 million

Annualized total returns: 15.73%, 3 years; 22.02%, 5 years; 21.02%, inception

Vanguard Equity-Income

Started: 1988

States available: All plus PR, GU, VI

Description: Seeks current income; capital appreciation potential among considerations. At least 80% of the fund's assets normally are invested in dividend-paying equity securities. Managers expect the average income yield of the portfolio to be at least 50% higher than that of the S&P 500

Index. Other assets may be invested in cash and fixed-income securities.

Adviser: Vanguard Group

Address and phone: Vanguard Financial Center, P.O. Box 2600, Valley Forge, PA 19482; 800-662-7447; 610-669-1000

Portfolio managers: Roger D. Newell, Anthony E. Spare, Jeffrey A. Kigner, Melody P. Sarnell

Standard deviation: 8.03

Beta: 0.85

Alpha: 1.9

R squared: 75

Minimum: $3,000

Minimum reinvestment: $100

Sales charges: None

Expense ratio: 0.45

Turnover: 31%

Assets: $1102.8 million

Annualized total returns: 15.72%, 3 years; 16.23%, 5 years; 13.06%, inception

Specialty

Vanguard Specialized Health Care

Started: 1984

States available: All plus PR, GU, VI

Description: Seeks long-term capital growth. Managers normally invest at least 80% of the fund's assets in companies that develop, produce, or distribute products or services used in treating or preventing diseases. Biotechnology companies may be included in the portfolio.

Adviser: Wellington Management

Address and phone: Vanguard Financial Center, P.O. Box 2600, Valley Forge, PA 19482; 800-662-7447; 610-669-1000

Portfolio manager: Edward P. Owens

Standard deviation: 12.31

Beta: 1.01

Alpha: 3.9
R squared: 45
Minimum: $3,000
Minimum reinvestment: $100
Sales charges: None
Expense ratio: 0.40
Turnover: 25%
Assets: $1278.4 million
Annualized total returns: 19.08%, 3 years; 20.36%, 5 years; 19.95%, 10 years

T. Rowe Price Science & Technology

Started: 1987
States available: All plus PR
Description: Concentrates on long-term growth of capital. Current income is not an important consideration. The fund normally invests at least 65% of its assets in foreign and domestic industries including computers, software, electronics, telecomunications, defense, aerospace, and biotechnology. Holdings may include new and established companies.
Adviser: T. Rowe Price Associates
Address and phone: 100 East Pratt Street, Baltimore, MD 21202; 800-638-5660; 410-547-2308
Portfolio manager: Charles A. Morris
Standard deviation: 17.22
Beta: 1.23
Alpha: 15.3
R squared: 34
Minimum: $2,500
Minimum reinvestment: $100
Sales charges: None
Expense ratio: 1.01
Turnover: 130%
Assets: $2216.8 million

Annualized total returns: 34.03%, 3 years; 35.82%, 5 years; 23.10%, inception

Invesco Strategic Health Sciences
Started: 1984

States available: All plus PR, GU,VI

Description: The fund seeks capital appreciation. It normally invests 80% of assets in equity securities issued by companies engaged in the development, production, or distribution of products or services related to the health sciences. These may include companies engaged in the manufacture or sale of medical equipment, medical supplies, or pharmaceuticals, or companies that operate health-care facilities.

Adviser: Invesco Funds Group

Address and phone: P.O. Box 173708, Denver, CO 80217-3706; 800-525-8085

Portfolio manager: John R. Schroer

Standard deviation: 16.73

Beta: 0.92

Alpha: −1.7

R squared: 20

Minimum: $1,000

Minimum reinvestment: $50

Sales charges: None

Expense ratio: 1.19

Turnover: 80%

Assets: $861 million

Annualized total returns: 56.57%, 1 year; 25.42%, 3 years; 15.71%, 5 years; 22.95%, 10 years

Balanced

Dodge & Cox Balanced
Started: 1931

States available: All except NE, plus NR

Description: Seeks income, conservation of principal, and long-term growth of principal and income. Up to 75% of the fund's assets may be invested in common stocks and convertible securities, and in their purchase, prospective earnings and dividends are weighted heavily. Individual securities are considered on the merit of their financial strength and economic background. Other assets include investment-grade fixed-income securities. Unrated debt must be judged equivalent to those rated A or higher. Managers may hold securities that have been downgraded below BBB.
Adviser: Dodge & Cox
Address and phone: 1 Sansome Street, 35th Floor, San Francisco, CA 94104; 800-621-3979
Portfolio manager: Management team
Standard deviation: 6.55
Beta: 0.72
Alpha: 2.5
R Squared: 80
Minimum: $2,500
Minimum reinvestment: $100
Sales charges: None
Expense ratio: 0.57
Turnover: 20%
Assets: $1800.3 million
Annualized total returns: 14.85%, 3 years; 15.13%, 5 years; 13.56%, 10 years

Vanguard/Wellington
Started: 1929
States available: All plus PR, GU, VI
Description: Goals are conservation of capital and reasonable income. Sixty percent to 70% of the fund's assets typically are in common stocks. The rest may be in preferred stocks and debt securities. Up to 10% of the assets may be in foreign securities. Prior to May 3, 1993, the fund was named Wellington Fund.

Adviser: Wellington Management

Address and phone: Vanguard Financial Center, P.O. Box 2600, Valley Forge, PA 19482

Portfolio manager: Ernst H. von Metzsch

Standard deviation: 7.30

Beta: 0.82

Alpha: 1.1

R squared: 85

Minimum: $3,000

Minimum reinvestment: $100

Sales charges: None

Expense ratio: 0.35

Turnover: 32%

Assets: $12,656.0 million

Annualized total returns: 14.51%, 3 years; 14.91%, 5 years; 12.78%, 10 years

Invesco Balanced

Started: 1994

States available: All

Description: The fund seeks total return and typically invests 50% to 70% of its assets in common stocks and the balance in assets of fixed-income securities. At least 25% of assets are normally invested in U.S. government obligations and investment-grade corporate bonds. The fund may invest up to 25% of its assets directly in foreign securities; it may invest in ADRs without regard to this limitation. The fund may also invest in investment-grade municipal obligations. The average weighted maturity of the fixed-income portion varies according to market conditions.

Adviser: Invesco Funds Group

Address and phone: P.O. Box 173708, Denver, CO 80217-3706; 800-525-8085

Portfolio manager: Gerry Paul/Charles Mayer

Standard deviation: NA

Beta: NA
Alpha: NA
R squared: NA
Minimum: $1,000 or $50 a month
Minimum reinvestment: $50
Sales charges: None; 12b-1 fee, 0.25%
Expense ratio: 1.25
Turnover: 255%
Assets: $120 million
Annualized total returns: 33.92 percent, 1 year

Income

Lindner Dividend

Started: 1976

States available: All except AR, PR, GU

Description: Capital appreciation is secondary to current income. The fund invests in these securities, in order of preference: common stocks, preferred stocks convertible or not convertible into common stocks, corporate bonds, and debt securities issued or guaranteed by the U.S. government or its agencies. Electric and gas utilities may account for up to 40% of assets. Generally, no more than 35% of assets are in high-yield debt securities, but the fund reserves the right to exceed that percentage. The fund reopened to new investors in November 1993.

Adviser: Ryback Management

Address and phone: 7711 Carondelet, P.O. Box 11208, St. Louis, MO 63105; 314-727-5305

Portfolio manager: Eric E. Ryback

Standard deviation: 5.06

Beta: 0.50

Alpha: 0.7

R squared: 66

Minimum: $2,000

CHAPTER 5 The 33 Best Funds

Minimum reinvestment: $100
Sales charges: None
Expense ratio: 0.61
Turnover: 30%
Assets: $2088.5 million
Annualized total returns: 10.54%, 3 years, 15.81%, 5 years; 12.22%, 10 years

Vanguard/Wellesley Income

Started: 1970
States available: All plus PR, GU, VI
Description: Seeks current income consistent with reasonable risk. At least 65% of assets are invested in income-producing securities, including fixed-income securities and dividend-paying common stock. Fixed-income securities, which may include government and corporate bonds and preferred stock, usually account for about 60% of assets. Prior to May 3, 1993, the fund was named Wellesley Income Fund.
Adviser: Wellington Management
Address and phone: Vanguard Financial Center, P.O. Box 2600, Valley Forge, PA 19482; 800-662-7447; 610-669-1000
Portfolio manager: Earl E. McEvoy
Standard deviation: 6.53
Beta: 0.60
Alpha: 1.3
R squared: 57
Minimum: $3,000
Minimum reinvestment: $100
Sales charges: None
Expense ratio: 0.34
Turnover: 31%
Assets: $7180.7 million
Annualized total returns: 12.20%, 3 years; 13.29%, 5 years; 11.93%, 10 years

FIXED-INCOME FUNDS

Corporate Bond

Northeast Investors Trust
  Started: 1950
  States available: All plus PR
  Description: Capital appreciation is secondary to income. Primary investments include securities of established companies, including bonds, preferred stock, dividend-paying common stock, convertibles, and warrants. The portfolio generally has included debt securities rated below investment grade because the fund imposes no particular rating standards. The fund may borrow up to 25% of assets to make additional investments.
  Adviser: Northeast Investors Trustees
  Address and phone: 50 Congress Street, Boston, MA 02109; 800-225-6704; 617-523-3588
  Portfolio manager: Ernest E. Monrad
  Standard deviation: 5.88
  Beta: 0.73
  Alpha: 6.6
  R squared: 26
  Minimum: $1,000
  Minimum reinvestment: None
  Sales charges: None
  Expense ratio: 1.02
  Turnover: 41%
  Assets: $805.2 million
  Annualized total returns: 14.00%, 3 years; 17.07%, 5 years; 10.63%, 10 years

Strong Corporate Bond
  Started: 1985
  States available: All plus PR, GU
  Description: Seeks current income by investing in fixed-income securities and dividend-paying common

stocks. Fixed-income investments may include corporate debt securities, U.S. government-related obligations, bank obligations, and foreign securities. Common-stock investments usually consist of utilities equities. The fund may invest up to 25% of its assets in debt rated below investment grade. Prior to May 1, 1995, the fund was named Strong Income Fund.

Adviser: Strong Capital Management

Address and phone: P.O. Box 2936, Milwaukee, WI 53201-2936; 800-368-1030; 414-359-1400

Portfolio manager: Jeffery A. Koch

Standard deviation: 5.14

Beta: 1.19

Alpha: 4.0

R squared: 92

Minimum: $1,000

Minimum reinvestment: $50

Sales charges: None

Expense ratio: 1.00

Turnover: 603%

Assets: $283.6 million

Annualized total returns: 12.49%, 3 years; 12.49%, 5 years; 9.72%, 10 years

Government Bond

Strong Government Securities

Started: 1986

States available: All plus PR, GU

Description: Goal is current income. The fund normally invests at least 80% of its assets in U.S. government securities. In addition to Treasury obligations, these may include securities issued by the Federal Housing Administration, Government National Mortgage Association, Federal Home Loan banks, and the Student Loan Marketing Association. Other assets may include investment-grade fixed-income securities.

Adviser: Strong Funds Distributors
Address and phone: P.O. Box 2936, Milwaukee, WI 53201-2936; 800-368-1030; 414-359-1400
Portfolio manager: Bradley C. Tank
Standard deviation: 4.67
Beta: 1.07
Alpha: 0.4
R squared: 97
Minimum: $1,000
Minimum reinvestment: $50
Sales charges: None
Expense ratio: 0.90
Turnover: 479% (1994)
Assets: $541.9 million
Annualized total returns: 6.99%, 3 years; 9.98%, 5 years; 9.25%, inception

Vanguard Fixed Income GNMA

Started: 1980
States available: All plus PR, GU, VI
Description: Seeks current income consistent with safety of principal and maintenance of liquidity. At least 80% of the fund's assets normally are in Government National Mortgage Association certificates. Other assets are invested in U.S. government securities and repurchase agreements secured by U.S. government securities.
Adviser: Vanguard Group
Address and phone: Vanguard Financial Center, P.O. Box 2600, Valley Forge, PA 19482; 800-662-7447; 610-669-1000
Portfolio manager: Paul D. Kaplan
Standard deviation: 3.43
Beta: 0.73
Alpha: 0.1
R squared: 97
Minimum: $3,000

Minimum reinvestment: $100
Sales charges: None
Expense ratio: 0.30
Turnover: 35%
Assets: $6684.8 million
Annualized total returns: 6.78%, 3 years; 9.24%, 5 years; 9.40%, 10 years

International/Global Bond

T. Rowe Price International Bond

Started: 1986

States available: All plus PR

Description: In seeking income, invests largely in non-U.S.-dollar-denominated, fixed-income securities. Management of the fund's security structure relies on the interest rate outlook for each foreign country. It also may use futures, options, and forward foreign currency contracts.

Adviser: T. Rowe Price Investment Services

Address and phone: 100 East Pratt Street, Baltimore, MD 21202; 800-638-5660; 410-547-2308

Portfolio manager: Peter B. Askew

Standard deviation: 7.56

Beta: 0.58

Alpha: 4.9

R squared: 10

Minimum: $2,500

Minimum reinvestment: $100

Sales charges: None

Expense ratio: 0.99 (1994)

Turnover: 345% (1994)

Assets: $979.4 million

Annualized total returns: 11.01%, 3 years; 11.14%, 5 years; 10.54%, inception

Municipal Bond

Vanguard Municipal Intermediate

Started: 1977

States available: All plus PR, GU, VI

Description: Seeks income exempt from federal income tax, consistent with preservation of capital. Typically, 65% of assets are in municipal securities. At least 95% of these securities are usually rated BBB or above. At least 80% are rated A or better. The fund may invest in short-term municipal obligations. It usually does not invest in securities subject to the Alternative Minimum Tax.

Adviser: Vanguard Group

Address and phone: Vanguard Financial Center, P.O. Box 2600, Valley Forge, PA 19482; 800-662-7447; 610-669-1000

Portfolio manager: Ian A. MacKinnon

Standard deviation: 4.52

Beta: 0.81

Alpha: 0.3

R squared: 56

Minimum: $3,000

Minimum reinvestment: $100

Sales charges: None

Expense ratio: 0.21

Turnover: 12%

Assets: $5724.0 million

Annualized total returns: 7.61%, 3 years; 8.58%, 5 years; 8.83%, 10 years

Vanguard Municipal Insured Long-Term

Started: 1984

States available: All plus PR, GU, VI

Description: Seeks income exempt from federal income tax. Normally has at least 80% of assets in insured tax-free municipal securities. The balance may be invested in municipal bonds rated A or better. The fund generally maintains an average weighted maturity of 15 to 25 years. Managers expect overall quality of the portfolio to be AAA.

Adviser: Vanguard Group

Address and phone: Vanguard Financial Center, P.O. Box 2600, Valley Forge, PA 19482; 800-662-7447; 610-669-1000

Portfolio manager: Ian A. MacKinnon

Standard deviation: 6.92

Beta: 1.29

Alpha: -0.9

R squared: 61

Minimum: $3,000

Minimum reinvestment: $100

Sales charges: None

Expense ratio: 0.21

Turnover: 7%

Assets: $2006.0 million

Annualized total returns: 8.18%, 3 years; 9.00%, 5 years; 9.53%, 10 years

CHAPTER 6

The 27 Runners-Up

A good number of clearly superior funds did not make the elite list of 33. Some of these spurned funds were, perhaps, all-too-obvious choices: Fidelity Magellan, for example, one of the best-performing funds ever. Other notable funds totally ignored by our panelists include: Twentieth Century Giftrust, Vanguard/Windsor, Fidelity Destiny 1 and 2, and Sequoia. (If a sports authority is asked to name the greatest player who ever lived, he or she doesn't say Babe Ruth or Hank Aaron. Authorities aren't expected to give obvious answers.)

Other fine funds may have been overlooked because a decision had to be made, so almost any excuse would serve to eliminate certain contestants. Maybe Perkins Opportunity and Van Wagoner funds were brushed aside because they are considered just too young and sassy. And perhaps our experts were bored with reading about such ancient warhorses as Acorn and Harbor International, just as an ancient Greek voted against Aristides the Just because he was tired of hearing him always called "the Just."

Whatever the reasons for their omission, it's appropriate to list these also-rans—funds that received at least two nominations. They warrant being mentioned because an investor may already own shares of some of them and want reassurance that they remain good choices. Besides, an investor may prefer a fund on this list of also-rans to one on the very top list. Perhaps a fund is a member of a family that an investor already belongs to, so switching from fund to fund, or tacking on another fund, would be easy.

The 47 also-rans in the previous poll included these funds that did not make either of this poll's lists: Acorn, Alger Small Cap, Babson Enterprise, Columbia Special, Founders Discovery, Montgomery Small Cap, Nicholas Limited, Lindner, Vanguard/Windsor II, Berger 100, Fidelity Disciplined Equity, Gabelli Growth, Value Line Leveraged Growth, Franklin Rising Dividends, Fidelity Fund, Fidelity Europe, T. Rowe Price New Asia, Fidelity Utilities Income, Cohen & Steers Realty, Fidelity Puritan, Fidelity Asset Manager, Twentieth Century Balanced, USAA Mutual Income, Value Line Income, Income Fund of America, Fidelity Capital and Income, Fidelity Short-Term Bond, Invesco High Yield Bond, Janus Flexible Income, T. Rowe Price New Income, Scudder Income, Vanguard High Yield Bond, Benham GNMA & Income, Invesco Intermediate, Blanchard Short-Term Global, Alliance Short-Term, Fidelity High-Income Muni, Fidelity Limited Term Muni, and Vanguard Muni High Yield.

The message seems to be that it's hard to vote for a fund that hasn't been shooting out all the lights lately. On the other hand, funds like Janus Flexible have continued to do well—and yet received no votes from anyone. Perhaps the high attrition rate among the also-rans from the earlier poll to this poll is simply due to the proliferation of funds. Of course, it's also true that the earlier list contained 93 funds (47 top funds and 46 also-rans), and this poll's lists contain only 60—33 on the top list and 27 on the list of also-rans.

Following are the 27 funds that received two votes from the panelists, followed by details about these funds.

STOCKS

Aggressive growth

1. Brandywine
2. Kaufmann
3. Stein Roe Capital Opportunities
4. Warburg Pincus Emerging Growth

CHAPTER 6   The 27 Runners-Up

Small Company
5. Artisan Small Cap
6. Fidelity Low-Priced Stock
7. Heartland Value
8. T. Rowe Price New Horizons

Growth
9. Janus
10. Strong Opportunity
11. Yacktman

Growth and Income
12. Baron Growth & Income

International/Global
13. Lexington Worldwide Emerging
14. Colonial Newport Tiger
15. Oakmark International
16. SoGen International
17. Templeton Foreign

Equity Income
18. Fidelity Equity-Income

Specialty
19. Fidelity Health Care

Balanced
The three leaders among the top 33 funds dominated the field. Balanced funds receiving one vote were CGM Mutual, Dreyfus Balanced, Fidelity Balanced, Fidelity Puritan, Strong Total Return, and Vanguard Asset Allocation.

Income
20. T. Rowe Price Spectrum Income

Corporate Bond
21. Loomis-Sayles Bond

22. T. Rowe Price High Yield
23. Vanguard Long-Term Corporate

Government Bond
24. Harbor Bond

Municipal Bond
25. Vanguard Limited-Term Municipal

International/Global Bond
26. PIMCO Foreign Institutional
27. Scudder Emerging Markets Income

Here are brief profiles of those brave funds that also ran:

Aggressive growth

Brandywine
Started: 1985
States available: All
Description: Seeks long-term capital appreciation. Current income is secondary. Managers invest largely in common stocks of well-financed companies. Such stocks are likely issues of small, lesser-known companies moving to a higher market share. The fund also may invest in stocks of larger, better-researched companies.
Adviser: Friess Associates
Address and phone: P.O. Box 4166, Greenville, DE 19807; 800-656-3017; 302-656-6200
Portfolio manager: Foster S. Friess
Standard deviation: 13.99
Beta: 0.98
Alpha: 2.3
R squared: 33
Minimum: $25,000
Minimum reinvestment: $1,000
Sales charges: None

Expense ratio: N.A.
Turnover: N.A.
Assets: $4489.7 million
Annualized total returns: 17.98%, 3 years; 21.01%, 5 years; 18.46%, 10 years

Kaufmann

Started: 1986
States available: All except NE
Description: Seeks long-term capital appreciation by investing primarily in common stocks of small- and medium-size companies. The fund also may purchase convertibles. Portfolio candidates are evaluated according to growth prospects, economic outlook for the industry, product development, management, and security value. The fund may invest up to 10% of its assets in options and may leverage up to one-third of its holdings.
Adviser: Edgemont Asset Management
Address and phone: 140 E. 45th St., 43rd Floor, New York, NY 10017; 800-237-0132; 212-922-0123
Portfolio managers: Lawrence Auriana, Hans Utsch
Standard deviation: 14.00
Beta: 1.04
Alpha: 5.1
R squared: 36
Minimum: $1,500
Minimum reinvestment: $100
Sales charges: 0.75%
Expense ratio: 2.17
Turnover: 60%
Assets: $3159.8 million
Annualized total returns: 20.73%, 3 years; 28.58%, 5 years; 17.92%, 10 years

Stein Roe Capital Opportunities

Started: 1969

States available: All plus PR, GU, VI

Description: Concentrates on common stocks in its quest for long-term capital appreciation. The fund also may invest in all variety of equity and debt securities. The portfolio may include investments in securities of established companies and smaller, newer companies judged to have potential for rapid earnings growth. Up to 35% of the fund's assets may be in debt securities.

Adviser: Stein Roe & Farnham

Address and phone: P.O. Box 804058, Chicago, IL 60680; 800-338-2550; 312-368-7800

Portfolio manager: Gloria J. Santella

Standard deviation: 13.55

Beta: 1.05

Alpha: 7.9

R squared: 40

Minimum: $2,500

Minimum reinvestment: $100

Sales charges: None

Expense ratio: 1.05

Turnover: 0.08%

Assets: $332.5 million

Annualized total returns: 24.35%, 3 years; 26.24%, 5 years; 14.34%, 10 years

Warburg Pincus Emerging Growth

Started: 1988

States available: All plus PR

Description: Pursues capital appreciation. The fund normally invests at least 65% of its assets in common stocks of small- and medium-size companies that show positive earnings and prospects of achieving significant growth in a short period of time. Up to 20% of its assets may be in investment-grade debt securities. Up to 10% of its assets may be in foreign securities. Prior to February 26, 1992, the fund was named Counsellors Emerging Growth Fund.

Adviser: Warburg Pincus Counsellors
Address and phone: 466 Lexington Avenue, New York, NY 10017; 800-257-5614
Portfolio managers: Elizabeth B. Dater, Stephen J. Lurito
Standard deviation: 12.73
Beta: 0.97
Alpha: 4.4
R squared: 39
Minimum: $2,500
Minimum reinvestment: $100
Sales charges: None
Expense ratio: 1.26
Turnover: 85%
Assets: $515.1 million
Annualized total returns: 19.41%, 3 years; 24.42%, 5 years; 18.39%, inception

Small Company

Artisan Small Cap

Started: 1995
States available: All plus PR
Description: Seeks long-term capital growth. The fund normally invests at least 65% of assets in small companies with capitalizations of less than $1 billion. Managers place large emphasis on research and meet personally with company management when considering investing. The portfolio is likely to include stocks that are selling at substantial discounts to their estimated value. No more than 25% of the fund's assets may be in foreign securities, including American depositary receipts.
Adviser: Artisan Partners
Address and phone: 1000 North Water Street, Suite 1770, Milwaukee, WI 53202; 800-344-1770
Portfolio manager: Carlene Murphy Ziegler
Standard deviation: N.A.

Beta: N.A.
Alpha: N.A.
R squared: N.A.
Minimum: $1,000
Minimum reinvestment: $50
Sales charges: None
Expense ratio: 2.00
Turnover: N.A.
Assets: $249.7 million
Annualized total returns: 47.86%, inception

Fidelity Low-Priced Stock

Started: 1989

States available: All

Description: Seeks capital apprecation by normally investing at least 65% of assets in equity securities that are trading at $25 per share or less. The portfolio may include securities that have appreciated beyond that level. The fund's low-priced stocks are considered to be undervalued. Often the issuing companies have market capitalizations of less than $100 million; some have a negative net worth.

Adviser: Fidelity Management & Research

Address and phone: 82 Devonshire Street, Boston, MA 02109; 800-544-8888

Portfolio manager: Joel C. Tillinghast

Standard deviation: 8.08

Beta: 0.72

Alpha: 4.7

R squared: 52

Minimum: $2,500

Minimum reinvestment: $250

Sales charges: 3.00%

Expense ratio: 1.11

Turnover: 65%

Assets: $3277.0 million

Annualized total returns: 15.84%, 3 years; 23.98%, 5 years; 19.01%, inception

Heartland Value

Started: 1984

States available: All plus PR

Description: Goal is long-term capital appreciation. Managers normally invest at least 65% of assets in equities of companies with market capitalizations of less than $300 million. The fund emphasizes securities that are underpriced relative to price/earnings, price/book, price/cash-flow ratios, earnings growth, long-term debt/capital, and dividend stability. Up to 5% of the fund's assets may be in both convertibles and warrants. Up to 15% of assets may be in foreign securities.

Adviser: Heartland Advisors

Address and phone: 790 North Milwaukee Street, Milwaukee, WI 53202; 800-432-7856; 414-347-7777

Portfolio manager: William J. Nasgovitz

Standard deviation: 9.29

Beta: 0.62

Alpha: 6.4

R squared: 29

Minimum: Shut

Minimum reinvestment: Shut

Sales charges: 0.25%

Expense ratio: N.A.

Turnover: N.A.

Assets: $1173.9 million

Annualized total returns: 17.62%, 3 years; 27.94%, 5 years; 16.03%, 10 years

T. Rowe Price New Horizons

Started: 1960

States available: All plus PR

Description: Seeks capital apprecation by investing primarily in common stocks of small, rapidly growing companies. Up to 10% of the fund's assets may be in securities traded primarily outside the United States.

Adviser: T. Rowe Price Associates

Address and phone: 100 East Pratt Street, Baltimore, MD 21202; 800-638-5660; 410-547-2308

Portfolio manager: John H. Laporte

Standard deviation: 13.75

Beta: 1.10

Alpha: 7.1

R squared: 42

Minimum: Shut to new investors

Minimum reinvestment: Shut

Sales charges: None

Expense ratio: 0.90

Turnover: 56%

Assets: $2763.1 million

Annualized total returns: 23.91%, 3 years; 26.20%, 5 years; 14.46%, 10 years

Janus

Started: 1970

States available: All plus PR, GU, VI

Description: Seeks capital appreciation. Invests mainly in companies with increasing demand for their products or that operate in a favorable regulatory climate. The fund may invest without limit in foreign securities.

Adviser: Janua Capital

Address and phone: 100 Fillmore St., Suite 300, Denver, CO 80206-4923; (800) 525-8983

Portfolio manager: James P. Craig

Standard deviation: 7.53

Beta: 0.85

Alpha: –0.7

R squared: 87

CHAPTER 6 The 27 Runners-Up

Minimum: $2,500
Minimum reinvestment: $100
Sales charges: None
Expense ratio: 0.86
Turnover: 118%
Assets: $12,466 million
Annualized total returns: 14.8%, 3 years; 14.45%, 5 years; 14.84%, 10 years

Strong Opportunity

Started: 1985

States available: All plus PR, GU

Description: The fund normally invests at least 70% of assets in equities, including common stocks, convertible debentures, preferred stocks, convertible preferred stocks, and warrants in its quest for capital appreciation. Other assets may be in nonconvertible corporate and government intermediate- to long-term debt securities. Up to 15% of the fund's assets may be in foreign securities.

Adviser: Strong Capital Management

Address and phone: P.O. Box 2936, Milwaukee, WI 53201-2936; 800-368-1030; 414-359-1400

Portfolio manager: Richard T. Weiss, Marina T. Carlson

Standard deviation: 9.21
Beta: 0.88
Alpha: 1.7
R squared: 61
Minimum: $1,000
Minimum reinvestment: $50
Sales charges: None
Expense ratio: 1.3
Turnover: 93%
Assets: $1386.2 million
Annualized total returns: 16.56%, 3 years; 19.32%, 5 years; 17.79%, 10 years

Yacktman

Started: 1992

States available: All

Description: Current income is secondary to long-term growth of capital. Managers invest primarily in equities. Limits are not placed on the percentage of assets in any particular type of security. The fund focuses on companies with at least $1 billion in market capitalization.

Adviser: Yacktman Asset Management

Address and phone: 303 West Madison Street, Chicago, IL 60606; 800-525-8258; 312-201-1200

Portfolio manager: Donald A. Yacktman

Standard deviation: 10.42

Beta: 0.91

Alpha: –2.8

R squared: 52

Minimum: $2,500

Minimum reinvestment: $100

Sales charges: 0.25%

Expense ratio: 0.91

Turnover: 55%

Assets: $607.1 million

Annualized total returns: 29.62%, 1 year; 11.67%, 3 years; 10.53%, inception

Growth and Income

Baron Growth & Income

Started: 1994

States available: All except AK, OH, TX

Description: Income is secondary to capital appreciation. Managers invest in equity and debt securities. The equity portion consists mainly of common stocks and stock-related investments issued by companies with market capitalizations of $100 million to $1.5 billion. Up to 25% of the fund's assets may be in debt securities rated below investment grade. Up to 10% of its assets may be in foreign securities.

Adviser: Baron Capital

Address and phone: 450 Park Avenue, Suite 2802, New York, NY 10022; 800-992-2766; 212-759-7700

Portfolio manager: Ronald Baron

Standard deviation: N.A.

Beta: N.A.

Alpha: N.A.

R squared: N.A.

Minimum: $2,000

Minimum reinvestment: None

Sales charges: 0.25%

Expense ratio: 2.0

Turnover: N.A.

Assets: $64.2 million

Annualized total returns: 47.69%, 1 year; 50.87%, inception

International/Global

Lexington Worldwide Emerging Markets

Started: 1969

States available: All

Description: Goal is long-term growth of capital. At least 65% of the fund's assets are in emerging-country and emerging-market equity securities. The fund may enter into foreign-exchange contracts to hedge against currency rise. Prior to June 14, 1991, the fund was named Lexington Growth Fund.

Adviser: Lexington Management

Address and phone: P.O. Box 1515, Park 80 West Plaza Two, Saddle Brook, NJ 07662; 800-526-0057; 201-845-7300

Portfolio manager: Richard T. Saler

Standard deviation: 17.81

Beta: 0.92

Alpha: −2.8
R squared: 17
Minimum: $1,000
Minimum reinvestment: $50
Sales charges: None
Expense ratio: 1.88
Turnover: 93%
Assets: $253.4 million
Annualized total returns: 9.34%, 3 years; 12.98%, 5 years; 10.56%, 10 years

Colonial Newport Tiger T

Started: 1989
States available: All plus PR
Description: Seeks capital appreciation. Invests mainly in stocks in Hong Kong, Singapore, South Korea, Taiwan, and other nations of Southeast Asia. Seeks companies able to adapt to changes.
Adviser: Newport Fund Management
Address and phone: 1 Financial Center, Boston, MA 02111; 800-248-2828
Portfolio manager: John M. Mussey
Standard deviation: 22.42
Beta: 1.25
Alpha: 4.3
R squared: 21
Minimum: Shut to new investors
Minimum reinvestment: Shut
Sales charges: 5.75%
Expense ratio: 1.49
Turnover: 4%
Assets: $208 million
Annualized total returns: 17.02%, 3 years; 19.16%, 5 years

Oakmark International

Started: 1992

States available: All

Description: Seeks long-term capital appreciation. At least 65% of the fund's investments may be in foreign securities considered undervalued relative to their underlying economic value. Managers examine a company's ability to generate cash flow, quality of management, market share, and degree of pricing power. Up to 10% of assets may be in low-quality debt.

Adviser: Harris Associates

Address and phone: 2 North LaSalle Street, Chicago, IL 60602; 800-625-3790

Portfolio manager: David G. Herro

Standard deviation: 14.16

Beta: 1.01

Alpha: 0.3

R squared: 32

Minimum: $2,500

Minimum reinvestment: $100

Sales charges: None

Expense ratio: 1.4

Turnover: 27%

Assets: $907.9 million

Annualized total returns: −3.06%, 1 year; 14.36%, 3 years; 13.20%, inception

SoGen International

Started: 1970

States available: All plus PR

Description: Seeks long-term growth of capital and income. The fund invests largely in foreign and domestic common stocks and convertibles. Fixed-income assets may be included if they illustrate potential for capital appreciation. The fund may purchase debt on which the issuer has defaulted.

Adviser: Societe Generale Asset Management

Address and phone: 1221 Avenue of the Americas, 8th Floor, New York, NY 10020; 800-628-0252; 212-278-5800

Portfolio manager: Jean-Marie Eveillard
Standard deviation: 5.43
Beta: 0.41
Alpha: 5.2
R squared: 36
Minimum: $1,000
Minimum reinvestment: $100
Sales charges: 3.75%
Expense ratio: 1.26
Turnover: 13%
Assets: $2613.3 million
Annualized total returns: 12.79%, 3 years; 12.92%, 5 years; 13.18%, 10 years

Templeton Foreign

Started: 1982
States available: All plus PR
Description: Seeks long-term capital growth by investing largely in stocks and debt securities of companies and governments outside the United States. Up to 5% of the fund's assets may be in medium- or lower-quality debt securities.
Adviser: Templeton Galbraith & Hansberger
Address and phone: 700 Central Avenue, St. Petersburg, FL 33701; 800-292-9293; 813-823-8712
Portfolio manager: Mark G. Holowesko
Standard deviation: 9.60
Beta: 0.71
Alpha: 3.1
R squared: 35
Minimum: $100
Minimum reinvestment: $25
Sales charges: 5.75%
Expense ratio: 1.15
Turnover: 22%

CHAPTER 6 The 27 Runners-Up

Assets: $6936.5 million
Annualized total returns: 12.56%, 3 years; 10.41%, 5 years; 15.95%, 10 years

Equity Income

Fidelity Equity-Income

Started: 1966
States available: All
Description: Seeks income and capital appreciation. At least 65% of the fund's assets may be in income-producing equity securities whose demonstrated yield is higher than the composite yield on the stocks in the S&P 500 Index. Other assets may be in debt obligations, including convertible securities.
Adviser: Fidelity Management & Research
Address and phone: 82 Devonshire Street, Boston, MA 02109; 800-544-8888
Portfolio manager: Stephen R. Petersen
Standard deviation: 7.95
Beta: 0.88
Alpha: 2.7
R squared: 82
Minimum: $2,500
Minimum reinvestment: $250
Sales charges: 2.00%
Expense ratio: 0.69
Turnover: 50%
Assets: $10492.1 million
Annualized total returns: 16.25%, 3 years; 18.44%, 5 years; 12.87%, 10 years

Specialty

Fidelity Select Health Care

Started: 1981
States available: All

Description: Seeks capital appreciation. At least 80% of the fund's assets are in equity securities of companies in the health-care industry. The fund may invest up to 25% of assets in securities of one issuer and up to 5% of assets in lower-quality bonds.
Adviser: Fidelity Management & Research
Address and phone: 82 Devonshire Street, Boston, MA 02109; 800-544-8888
Portfolio manager: Karen Firestone
Standard deviation: 14.29
Beta: 0.90
Alpha: 5.8
R squared: 26
Minimum: $2,500
Minimum reinvestment: $250
Sales charges: 3.00%
Expense ratio: 1.36
Turnover: 151%
Assets: $1313.6 million
Annualized total returns: 18.36%, 3 years; 21.25%, 5 years; 19.89%, 10 years

Balanced

The three leaders—Dodge & Cox Balanced, Vanguard/Wellington, and Invesco Balanced—dominated the field. Balanced funds receiving one vote were CGM Mutual, Dreyfus Balanced, Fidelity Balanced, Fidelity Puritan, Strong Total Return, and Vanguard Asset Allocation (not strictly a balanced fund).

Income

T. Rowe Price Spectrum Income
Started: 1990
States available: All plus PR
Description: Goal is current income and preservation of capital. Managers invest in T. Rowe Price mutual funds that

invest primarily in fixed-income securities, including the Equity-Income Fund and the International Bond Fund as well as other T. Rowe Price funds.

Adviser: T. Rowe Price Investment Services

Address and phone: 100 East Pratt Street, Baltimore, MD 21202; 800-638-5660; 410-547-2308

Portfolio manager: Peter Van Dyke

Standard deviation: 3.82

Beta: 0.36

Alpha: 1.3

R squared: 62

Minimum: $2,500

Minimum reinvestment: $100

Sales charges: None

Expense ratio: 0.0

Turnover: 20%

Assets: $959.1 million

Annualized total returns: 9.58%, 3 years, 11.17%, 5 years; 10.61%, inception

Corporate Bond

Loomis-Sayles Bond

Started: 1991

States available: All plus PR

Description: Seeks total return in current income and capital appreciation. At least 65% of the fund's assets normally are in investment-grade debt securities, including convertibles. Other assets may be in securities rated below BBB. Up to 20% of the fund's assets may be in preferred stocks. It may invest without limit in Canadian issues and may invest up to 20% of assets in securities issued in foreign countries.

Adviser: Loomis Sayles

Address and phone: 1 Financial Center, Boston, MA 02111; 800-633-3330; 617-482-2450

Portfolio manager: Daniel J. Fuss

Standard deviation: 6.33
Beta: 1.31
Alpha: 6.0
R squared: 76
Minimum: $2,500
Minimum reinvestment: $50
Sales charges: None
Expense ratio: 0.79
Turnover: 35%
Assets: $252.4 million
Annualized total returns: 31.96%, 1 year; 15.66%, 3 years; 14.89%, inception

T. Rowe Price High Yield

Started: 1984
States available: All plus PR
Description: Growth of capital is secondary to high current income. The fund normally invests at least 80% of assets in high-yield, income-producing debt and preferred stocks. Up to 20% of assets may be in both foreign securities and common stocks. Average portfolio maturity is expected to be 10 years. Pacific Horizon High-Yield Bond and Security Income Fund High-Yield merged into this fund in March and December 1991.
Adviser: T. Rowe Price Associates
Address and phone: 100 East Pratt Street, Baltimore, MD 21202; 800-638-5660; 410-547-2308
Portfolio manager: Catherine H. Bray
Standard deviation: 5.77
Beta: 0.81
Alpha: 1.7
R squared: 34
Minimum: $2,500
Minimum reinvestment: $100
Sales charges: None
Expense ratio: 0.88

Turnover: 74%
Assets: $1226.6 million
Annualized total returns: 9.07%, 3 years; 14.27%, 5 years; 9.11%, 10 years

Vanguard Long-Term Corporate
Started: 1973
States available: All plus PR, GU, VI
Description: Seeks current income consistent with maintenance of principal and liquidity. At least 70% of assets typically are in high-quality corporate bonds. The average weighted maturity is 15 to 25 years. Prior to October 28, 1991, the fund was named Vanguard Fixed-Income Securities Investment Grade Bond. From that date until November 1, 1993, the fund was named Vanguard Fixed-Income Securities Investment Grade Corporate Portfolio.
Adviser: Wellington Management
Address and phone: Vanguard Financial Center, P.O. Box 2600, Valley Forge, PA 19482; 800-662-7447; 610-669-1000
Portfolio manager: Earl E. McEvoy
Standard deviation: 6.43
Beta: 1.52
Alpha: 0.8
R squared: 99
Minimum: $3,000
Minimum reinvestment: $100
Sales charges: None
Expense ratio: 0.31
Turnover: 49%
Assets: $3356.1 million
Annualized total returns: 10.12%, 1 year; 12.46%, 5 years; 10.75%, 10 years

Government Bond

Harbor Bond
Started: 1987

States available: All plus PR

Description: Seeks total return consistent with preservation of capital. At least 65% of assets are in high-quality domestic or foreign obligations, including those issued by governments, supernational organizations, and corporations. The fund aims to maintain a portfolio duration of three to six years.

Adviser: Harbor Capital Advisors

Address and phone: 1 SeaGate, Toledo, OH 43666; 800-422-1050; 419-247-2477

Portfolio manager: William H. Gross

Standard deviation: 4.18

Beta: 0.93

Alpha: 1.0

R squared: 88

Minimum: $2,000

Minimum reinvestment: $500

Sales charges: None

Expense ratio: 0.70

Turnover: 89%

Assets: $233.4 million

Annualized total returns: 8.83%, 3 years; 10.97%, 5 years; 10.31%, inception

Municipal Bond

Vanguard Municipal Limited-Term

Started: 1987

States available: All plus PR, GU, VI

Description: Goal is income exempt from federal income tax, consistent with preservation of capital. Managers invest primarily in tax-exempt municipal obligations. At least 95% of such holdings are rated A or better. The fund expects to maintain an average weighted maturity of two to five years.

Adviser: Vanguard's Fixed-Income Group

CHAPTER 6 The 27 Runners-Up

Address and phone: Vanguard Financial Center, P.O. Box 2600, Valley Forge, PA 19482; 800-662-7447; 610-669-1000
Portfolio manager: Ian A. MacKinnon
Standard deviation: 1.97
Beta: 0.36
Alpha: –0.6
R squared: 62
Minimum: $3,000
Minimum reinvestment: $100
Sales charges: None
Expense ratio: 0.21
Turnover: 35%
Assets: $1685.2 million
Annualized total returns: 4.89%, 3 years; 6.12%, 5 years

International/Global Bond

PIMCO Foreign Institutional
Started: 1992
States available: All except AK, AZ, IA, ND, SD, WY
Description: Normally invests at least 85% in fixed-income securities in at least three foreign countries.
Adviser: Pacific Investment Management
Address and phone: 840 Newport Center Drive, Suite 360, Newport Beach, CA 92660; 800-800-0952
Portfolio managers: John L. Hague, Lee R. Thomas
Standard deviation: 5.54
Beta: 0.83
Alpha: 3.0
R squared: 42
Minimum: $1 million
Minimum reinvestment: None
Sales charges: None
Expense ratio: 0.47

Turnover: 299%
Assets: $258 million
Annualized total returns: 9.51%, 3 years

Scudder Emerging Markets Income

Started: 1993
States available: All
Description: Normally invests at least 65% of assets in high-yielding debt securities in emerging markets, primarily in Latin America.
Adviser: Scudder Stevens & Clark
Address and phone: 2 International Place, Boston, MA 02110; 800-225-2470; 617-439-4640
Portfolio manager: Susan E. Gray
Standard deviation: NA
Beta: NA
Alpha: NA
R squared: NA
Minimum: $1,000
Minimum reinvestment: $100
Sales charges: None
Expense ratio: 1.5
Turnover: 302%
Assets: $222 million
Annualized total returns: 31.43%, 1 year

CHAPTER 7

The Single Best Fund

There were a few clear-cut winners in the voting for "single best fund." The top vote-getters were the similar Mutual Series funds, Shares, Beacon, and Qualified, with four votes (Humphries, Litman, Markman, Weber). The funds were recently sold to the Franklin family.

Runner-up was Vanguard Index 500, with three nominations: from Pope, Berry, and Droms. Mutual Discovery added to Michael Price's glory, capturing two votes (Boroson, Stein). Two other funds were tied with two votes: Vanguard/Wellington (Brouwer, Savage) and T. Rowe Price Equity-Income (Schabacker, Higgins). The T. Rowe Price fund was the very top vote-getter in the poll for best mutual fund. Mutual Qualified/Beacon and Vanguard Index Trust 500 were repeaters from 1993.

Dropping off the list were Fidelity Asset Manager, Fidelity Equity-Income II, Fidelity Balanced, Gateway Index Plus, Lindner, Lindner Dividend, Neuberger & Berman Guardian, Pennsylvania Mutual, and Yacktman. The performances of some of these funds faltered—Gateway Index Plus, for example, along with Pennsylvania Mutual. But Fidelity Equity-Income II and Lindner Dividend were elected to the list of best mutual funds, and a few others have done well, such as Yacktman.

Funds that received single votes as the best conservative fund: Dodge & Cox Balanced (Skala), Flexfunds Muirfield (Merriman), Templeton Growth I (Phillips), Merger (Donoghue), and Vanguard/Windsor II (Kolluri).

Here are profiles of the funds not included among the 33 funds in Chapter 5 or the also-rans in Chapter 6:

FlexFunds Muirfield

Started: 1988

States available: Various

Description: The fund invests in other mutual funds, sometimes even index funds.

Adviser: R. Meeder & Associates

Address and phone: 6000 Memorial Drive, Dublin, OH 43017; 800-325-3539

Portfolio manager: Robert S. Meeder Jr.

Standard deviation: 5.75

Beta: 0.41

Alpha: 4.3

R squared: 33

Minimum: $2,500

Minimum reinvestment: $100

Sales charges: 12b-1

Expense ratio: 1.26

Turnover: 186%

Assets: $122 million

Annualized total returns: 14.25%, 3 years; 11.85 %, 5 years

Templeton Growth I

Started: 1954

States available: All plus PR

Description: Invests mainly in common stocks, but has complete flexibility to invest in any kind of securities.

Adviser: Templeton Galbraith & Hansberger

Address and phone: 700 Central Avenue, St. Petersburg, FL 33706-3628; 800-292-9293
Portfolio manager: Mark G. Holowesko
Standard deviation: 9.54
Beta: 0.88
Alpha: 1.9
R squared: 57
Minimum: $100
Minimum reinvestment: $25
Sales charges: 5.75% load
Expense ratio: 1.12
Turnover: 35%
Assets: $7900 million
Annualized total returns: 15.67%, 3 years; 14.43%, 5 years; 12.75 %, 10 years

Merger

Started: 1989
States available: All
Description: Seeks capital appreciation. The fund normally invests at least 65% of assets in stocks of companies that are the objects of acquisitions or other reorganization proposals.
Adviser: Westchester Capital Management
Address and phone: 100 Summit Lake Drive, Valhalla, NY 10595; 800-343-8959
Portfolio manager: Frederick W. Green, Bonnie L. Smith
Standard deviation: 2.83
Beta: 0.10
Alpha: 6.8
R squared: 8
Minimum: Shut to new investors
Minimum reinvestment: Shut
Sales charges: 12b-1
Expense ratio: 1.41
Turnover: 419%

Assets: $296 million
Annualized total returns: 11.82%, 5 years

Vanguard/Windsor II
Started: 1985
States available: All plus PR, GU, VI
Description: Invests mainly in undervalued income-producing stocks with below-average price-earnings ratios compared with the market. Barrow, Hanley, Mewhinny & Struss supervises around 75% of the assets.
Adviser: Multiple
Address and phone: Vanguard Financial Center, P.O. Box 2600, Valley Forge, PA 19482; 800-662-7447
Portfolio manager: James P. Barrow
Standard deviation: 8.68
Beta: 0.98
Alpha: 0.4
R squared: 87
Minimum: $3,000
Minimum reinvestment: $100
Sales charges: None
Expense ratio: 0.39
Turnover: 30%
Assets: $11,760 million
Annualized total returns: 16.94%, 3 years; 15.05%, 5 years; 13.50%, 10 years

CHAPTER 8

The Single Best, Overlooked Fund

Asked to name a fund that few people are aware of, but should excel in the years to come, the panelists chose these:

Baron Asset (Markman)
Calvert Strategic Growth (Stein)
Dominion Insight Growth (Boroson)
Lexington Worldwide Emerging (Schabacker)
Merger (Humphries)
Merriman Leveraged Growth (Merriman)
PBHG Select Equity (Stein)
RCM Global Technologies Fund (Litman)
Robertson Stephens Contrarian (Droms)
Strong Growth (Weber)
Schwab 1000 (Weber)
Schooner (Phillips)
Third Avenue Value (Skala)
United Services Bonnell Growth (Donoghue)
Vontobel Europacific (Berry)
Warburg Pincus Japan OTC (Kolluri)

Not a single fund was named twice, although Merger also made the list of single best conservative funds. None of the funds were among the top 33 funds.

Some of these funds are truly tiny, but others—like Third Avenue Value and Baron Asset—are not exactly flowers wasting their fragrance on the desert air. Lexington Worldwide Emerging Markets is even on our list of runners-up! Not everyone voted. Pope's response: "I never touch [little-known funds]."

As for the little-known fine funds identified in our earlier poll, some of those funds deserved to remain obscure, especially American Heritage, which proceeded to disgrace itself. Also on that list were such unfortunates as Gateway Index Trust, Mathers, and Monetta.

But also on that list of little-known funds were such gems as Northeast Investors Trust, CGM Mutual, Harbor International, Lindner Dividend, Neuberger & Berman Guardian, PIMCO Low Duration, and T. Rowe Price Capital Appreciation. Northeast Investors Trust even made the list of top 33 funds this time around.

Here are details about the best overlooked funds that made this list, but not the list of top 33 funds or the list of runners-up.

Baron Asset
  Started: 1987
  States available: All plus PR
  Description: Seeks capital appreciation. The fund invests in companies between $100 million and $1.5 million in market capitalization; companies with apparently undervalued assets or favorable growth prospects. The fund looks for strong balance sheets, undervalued and unrecognized assets, low ratios of free cash flow and income, management skills, unit growth, and the potential to take advantage of economic trends. The fund may engage in short-term trading and in special situations.
  Adviser: BAMCO
  Address and phone: 450 Park Avenue, Suite 2802, New York, NY 10022; 800-992-2766
  Portfolio manager: Ronald Baron
  Standard deviation: 10.95

Beta: 0.87
Alpha: 10.4
R squared: 40
Minimum: $2,000
Minimum reinvestment: None
Sales charges: None
Expense ratio: 1.4
Turnover: 35%
Assets: $873 million
Annualized total returns: 22.31%, 5 years

Calvert Strategic Growth A
Started: 1994
States available: All
Description: Seeks long-term growth. Normally invests at least 65% of assets in stocks. Companies considered financially acceptable are screened for social responsibility vis-à-vis the environment, employee relations, and the manufacture of weapons and other harmful products. Up to 35% of assets may be invested in debt securities rated as low as C.
Adviser: Calvert Asset Management
Address and phone: P.O. Box 419544, Kansas City, MO 64141-6544; 800-368-2748
Portfolio manager: Cedd Moses
Standard deviation: NA
Beta: NA
Alpha: NA
R squared: NA
Minimum: $2,000
Minimum reinvestment: $250
Sales charges: 4.75%
Expense ratio: 2.55
Turnover: NA
Assets: $136 million
Annualized total returns: 29.14%, 1 year

Dominion Insight Growth
Started: 1992
States available: 36
Description: Small company, aggressive growth fund.
Adviser: OTC Capital
Address and phone: 800-880-1095
Portfolio manager: James O. Collins
Standard deviation: 20.68
Beta: 1.27
Alpha: 11.48
R squared: 24
Minimum: $5,000
Minimum reinvestment: $100
Sales charges: 3.5% load
Expense ratio: 2.38
Turnover: 210%
Assets: $20 million
Annualized total returns: 32.28%, 3 years

Merriman Leveraged Growth
Started: 1992
States available: 36
Description: Market-timed agressive growth fund.
Adviser: Merriman Investment Management
Address and phone: 800-423-4893
Portfolio manager: Merriman/Notaro
Standard deviation: 7.81
Beta: 0.58
Alpha: −0.79
R squared: 35
Minimum: $2,000
Minimum reinvestment: $100
Sales charges: None
Expense ratio: 2.82

CHAPTER 8   The Single Best, Overlooked Fund

Turnover: 88%
Assets: $16 million
Annualized total returns: 10.66%, 3 years

PBHG Select Equity

Started: 1995
States available: All
Description: Seeks long-term growth of capital. Normally invests 65% in the stocks of a small number of companies that seem to promise strong earnings growth. The fund may invest in foreign securities.
Adviser: Pilgrim Baxter & Associates
Address and phone: 680 E. Swedesford Road, Wayne, PA 19087-1658; 800-433-0051
Portfolio manager: Gary L. Pilgrim, James McCall
Standard deviation: NA
Beta: NA
Alpha: NA
R squared: NA
Minimum: $2,500
Minimum reinvestment: None
Sales charges: None
Expense ratio: 1.5
Turnover: 206%
Assets: $122 million
Annualized total returns: 95.89%, 1 year

RCM Global Technologies Fund

Started: 1995
States available: All
Description: Growth fund with at least 65% in technology stocks.
Adviser: RCM Capital Management
Address and phone: 800-726-7240
Portfolio manager: Chen/Price Jr.

Standard deviation: NA
Beta: NA
Alpha: NA
R squared: NA
Minimum: $25,000
Minimum reinvestment: NA
Sales charges: None
Expense ratio: NA
Turnover: NA
Assets: $2.9 million
Annualized total returns: NA

Robertson Stephens Contrarian
Started: 1993
States available: All except AK, MO, OH, WI
Description: Seeks long-term capital appreciation. Invests at least 65% of assets in stocks. Looks for undiscovered or out-of-favor companies. The fund is nondiversified.
Adviser: Robertson Stephens Investment Management
Address and phone: 555 California St., Suite 2600, San Francisco, CA 94104; (800) 766-3863
Portfolio manager: Paul H. Stephens
Standard deviation: NA
Beta: NA
Alpha: NA
R squared: NA
Minimum: $5,000
Minimum reinvestment: $100
Sales charges: 12b-1
Expense ratio: 2.54
Turnover: NA
Assets: $923 million
Annualized total returns: 26.22%, 1 year

Schooner
Started: 1993

CHAPTER 8 The Single Best, Overlooked Fund

States available: NA
Description: NA
Adviser: NA
Address and phone: 800-420-7556
Portfolio manager: Gipson/Grey
Standard deviation: NA
Beta: NA
Alpha: NA
R squared: NA
Minimum: $5,000
Minimum reinvestment: NA
Sales charges: None
Expense ratio: 1.5
Turnover: 40%
Assets: $5.9 million
Annualized total returns: 12.06%, 1 year

<u>Schwab 1000</u>

Started: 1991
States available: All plus PR
Description: Invests in the 1,000 largest publicly traded companies. Securities are not automatically bought and sold to reflect changes in the index.
Adviser: Charles Schwab Investment Management
Address and phone: 101 Montgomery St., San Francisco, CA 94104; 800-526-8600
Portfolio manager: Geraldine Horn
Standard deviation: 8.25
Beta: 0.98
Alpha: –0.4
R squared: 98
Minimum: $1,000
Minimum reinvestment: $100
Sales charges: None
Expense ratio: 0.54

Turnover: 2%
Assets: $1,270 million
Annualized total returns: 14.55%, 5 years

Strong Growth

Started: 1993
States available: All plus PR and GU
Description: Seeks capital appreciation. Normally invests 65% in stocks with above-average sales and earnings growth per share; high return on invested capital; good balance sheets, financial policies, and accounting methods; and overall financial strength.
Adviser: Strong Capital Management
Address and phone: P.O. Box 2936, Milwaukee, WI 53201-2936; 800-368-1030
Portfolio manager: Ronald C. Ognar
Standard deviation: NA
Beta: NA
Alpha: NA
R squared: NA
Minimum: $1,000
Minimum reinvestment: $50
Sales charges: None
Expense ratio: 1.6
Turnover: 386%
Assets: $685 million
Annualized total returns: 56.09%, 1 year

Third Avenue Value

Started: 1990
States available: All except AZ
Description: Seeks long-term capital appreciation. Invests mainly in stocks believed to be undervalued with strong financial positions and capable management.
Adviser: EQSF Advisers

CHAPTER 8   The Single Best, Overlooked Fund

Address and phone: 767 Third Avenue, Fifth Floor, New York, NY 10017; 800-443-1021
Portfolio manager: Martin J. Whitman
Standard deviation: 7.26
Beta: 0.68
Alpha: 2.3
R squared: 60
Minimum: $1,000
Minimum reinvestment: $1,000
Sales charges: None
Expense ratio: 1.25
Turnover: 15%
Assets: $328 million
Annualized total returns: 16.91%, 5 years

United Services Bonnel Growth

Started: 1994
States available: All
Description: Fund seeks long-term growth of capital by investing primarily in the common stock of mid-size growth companies. Invests in quality companies with strong earnings, low debt, dominance of market niche, and substantial equity ownership by management.
Adviser: U.S. Global Investors, Inc.
Address and phone: P.O. Box 781234, San Antonio, TX 78278-1234; 800-426-6635
Portfolio manager: Arthur J. Bonnel
Standard deviation: NA
Beta: NA
Alpha: NA
R squared: NA
Minimum: $5,000
Minimum reinvestment: $50
Sales charges: None
Expense ratio: 2.5

Turnover: 100%
Assets: $85 million
Annualized total returns: 63.95%, 1 year

Vontobel Europacific
Started: 1984
States available: All
Description: Seeks capital appreciation. Invests at least 65% of assets in stocks in Europe and the Pacific Basin.
Adviser: Vontobel USA
Address and phone: 1500 Forest Avenue, Suite 223, Richmond, VA 23229; 800-527-9500
Portfolio manager: Fabrizio Pieralini
Standard deviation: 12.84
Beta: 0.84
Alpha: 0.4
R squared: 28
Minimum: $1,000
Minimum reinvestment: $100
Sales charges: None
Expense ratio: 1.53
Turnover: 68%
Assets: $138 million
Annualized total returns: 7.09%, 10 years

Warburg Pincus Japan OTC
Started: 1994
States available: All except SD
Description: Seeks long-term capital appreciation. Normally invests at least 65% in Japanese over-the-counter stocks. The fund is nondiversified.
Adviser: Warburg Pincus Counsellors
Address and phone: 466 Lexington Ave., New York, NY 10017-3147; 800-927-2864
Portfolio manager: Shuhei Abe

Standard deviation: NA
Beta: NA
Alpha: NA
R squared: NA
Minimum: $2,500
Minimum reinvestment: $100
Sales charges: 12b-1
Expense ratio: 1.41
Turnover: 83%
Assets: $209 million
Annualized total returns: 32.55%, 1 year

CHAPTER 9

Most Admired Portfolio Managers

The panelists named the following as the most admired portfolio managers (number of nominations is in parentheses):

Michael Price (10)
Jeffrey Vinik (7)
Shelby Davis (4)
Robert Sanborn (3)
Ronald E. Elijah (2)
Foster Friess (2)
William Gross (2)

The portfolio manager our panelists admire the most is Michael Price, with 10 nominations. Jeffrey Vinik is in second place, with seven (this was before he left Fidelity Magellan). Price himself has sold his funds to the Franklin family but will remain at the Mutual Series funds for several years.

None of Shelby Davis's funds made our recommended list, presumably because they are load funds. Perhaps other managers of load funds, like Jack Murray, John Horseman, and Mark Mobius, would have received more nominations if they managed no-load funds.

Ruane probably received only one nomination because his fund has been closed for so long and because he is the opposite of a publicity seeker. But interestingly, he is the manager whom Michael Price has said that he admires most.

Sanborn's place on the list is impressive considering that he is a relative newcomer.

At least one panelist mentioned these managers: Arthur Bonnel, Hakan Castegren (Harbor International), James Gibson (Clipper), John Horseman (GAM International), Brad Lewis (Fidelity Disciplined Equity), Mark Mobius (Templeton Developing Markets), Ernest Monrad (Northeast Investors), Jack M. Mussey (Colonial Newport Tiger), Gary Pilgrim (PBHG), Brian Rogers (T. Rowe Price Equity-Income), William Ruane (Sequoia), John Wallace (Oppenheimer Growth and Income), Martin Whitman (Third Avenue Value), Donald Yacktman, Bonnie Smith (Merger), Ralph Wanger (Acorn), and Carlene Murphy Ziegler (Artisan).

Most-admired managers in the previous poll who dropped out include James Craig (Janus), Tom Marsico (Janus 20), and Mario Gabelli. While all these fund managers have had their ups and downs, they are pretty much up as of the current writing. But they have not recently enjoyed consecutive glittering years.

In the 1993 balloting, Michael Price received only one vote, as did Hakan Castegren, Robert Sanborn of Oakmark, Mark Mobius, Jeffrey Vinik, Ralph Wanger, and Donald Yacktman.

Others who received one vote are not heard from much these days: Henry van der Eb, Jr., of Mathers, Peter Thayer of Gateway Index Trust, William Sams of FPA Paramount, Heiko Thieme of American Heritage, Albert O. Nicholas, and the managers of the 20th Century funds. Some of these managers have fared poorly, like van der Eb and Thieme; others have done well, but not excited the popular imagination, like Sams and Nicholas.

Markman admires Price, Elijah, and Sanborn because "they exhibit intellectual courage and discipline, and that's what I look for, first and foremost, in a fund manager. They have the courage to act on their own convictions, not so much on what 'the Street' has concluded."

CHAPTER 9   Most Admired Portfolio Managers

Humphries says of Price, "I don't know how he does it, but his funds are consistently good, and without his taking much risk."

As for Shelby Davis, Savage admires his "consistent approach, strong work ethic, and very successful results. He embodies a lot of flexibility, and he's proved remarkably resilient in a variety of market environments."

Here are more details about funds managed by most-admired portfolio managers not already covered in other chapters. (Brandywine was described in Chapter 6, and so was Harbor Bond.)

Fidelity Magellan
  Started: 1963
  States available: All
  Description: The fund invests mainly in common stocks, focusing on domestic companies, companies with significant activities and interests outside the U.S., and foreign companies. It can invest up to 20% in debt securities.
  Adviser: Fidelity Management & Research
  Address and phone: 82 Devonshire St., Boston, MA 02109; 800-544-8888
  Portfolio manager: Robert E. Stansky
  Standard deviation: 11.11
  Beta: 1.03
  Alpha: 1.7
  R squared: 58
  Minimum: $2,500
  Minimum reinvestment: $250
  Sales charges: 3% load
  Expense ratio: 0.96
  Turnover: 120%
  Assets: $55 billion
  Annualized total returns: 14.77%, 3 years; 15.32%, 5 years; 14.98%, 10 years

Davis New York Venture A
Started: 1969
States available: All
Description: Seeks growth of capital and has a flexible charter.
Adviser: Davis Selected Advisers
Address and phone: 124 E. Marcy St., Santa Fe, NM 87501; 800-279-0279
Portfolio managers: Shelby M.C. Davis, Christopher C. Davis
Standard deviation: 11.24
Beta: 1.17
Alpha: −0.9
R squared: 73
Minimum: $1,000
Minimum reinvestment: $25
Sales charges: 4.75%
Expense ratio: 0.90
Turnover: 15%
Assets: $1.9 billion
Annualized total returns: 26.32%, 3 years; 17.59%, 5 years; 16.00%, 10 years

Robertson Stephens Value + Growth
Started: 1992
States available: All except AK, MO, OH, WI
Description: Typically investss 65% in stocks, focusing on mid-caps with low price–earnings ratios compared with their growth rates.
Adviser: Robertson Stephens Investment Management
Address and phone: 555 California St., Suite 2600, San Francisco, CA 94104; 800-766-3863
Portfolio manager: Ronald E. Elijah
Standard deviation: 16.56
Beta: 0.92
Alpha: 11.6

R squared: 21
Minimum: $5,000
Minimum reinvestment: $100
Sales charges: None
Expense ratio: 1.68
Turnover: 232%
Assets: $1,100 million
Annualized total returns: 27.34%, 3 years

CHAPTER 10

The Best Families

There are all sorts of rewards you get from buying funds in the same family:

- You can easily learn the general rules that apply to each fund—for example, what the minimum first investment is, the amount needed to reinvest, when distributions are made, how to withdraw funds, and so forth.
- Shifting between funds should be relatively easy; in some cases, a phone call will do. And even if the family is a load fund, you can move your existing funds around without new sales charges.
- The paperwork should be simpler than if you owned a variety of funds in different families.

Not that all of your funds need be in one family. If you stick with just a single family, you'll bypass some excellent funds, some of which may be virtual orphans (Clipper), some of which are members of undistinguished families (Dean Witter Dividend Growth), and some of which aren't by any definition part of a family (Acorn).

Still, if you're thinking of buying a particular kind of fund—growth, income, short-term bond—you should, other things being equal, keep it within a family you already have.

A fund family has been defined as a group of funds, under one umbrella, that includes at least one stock fund, one bond fund, and one money market fund.

The 19 panelists, asked to name their three favorite mutual fund families, named these most often in 1996 (the number of nominations follows each):

Vanguard (14)
Fidelity (10)
T. Rowe Price (8)
Mutual Series (5)
Strong (2)
Robertson Stephens (2)
American (2)
Morgan Stanley (2)
Oakmark (2)
Invesco (2)

There were single mentions of DFA, Harbor, Janus, Neuberger & Berman, PBHG, Putnam, Scudder, United Services, and Templeton.

Compared with the same poll three years ago, Vanguard has remained where it was, but Fidelity has leaped up to second place, after having been ensconced in fifth place. The Mutual Series funds weren't even on the 1993 list. No doubt the addition of Mutual Discovery has helped the family's reputation: Discovery differs from the other funds in its greater exposure to foreign and small-company stocks. Other newcomers to the top list: American, Morgan Stanley, Oakmark, and Robertson Stephens.

Falling off the 1993 list were Janus (from two votes to one), 20th Century (from five votes to none), Scudder (from three votes to one—and two votes as least admired family!). T. Rowe Price received the same number of votes both times; Invesco lost two; Strong captured one.

CHAPTER 10   The Best Families

A few newer families received recognition: Robertson Stephens, Morgan Stanley, and Oakmark.

The appearance of load funds on the list—American (Los Angeles), Putnam, and Templeton (Franklin)—is an impressive compliment, considering that most panelists strongly favor no-load funds.

Widely respected fund families that were overlooked include Acorn, Berger, Dodge & Cox, Founders, and Twentieth Century.

Skala praises Vanguard for its willingness to drop portfolio managers who underperform: "The managers have no long-term guarantees." (Not long ago, Vanguard discharged a noted money manager, Batterymarch, as adviser for its World Growth-U.S. fund.) Skala also admires the family for its awesomely low expenses: "And on the fixed-income side," he notes, "low expenses are almost the name of the game."

William Donoghue voted for Fidelity: "As marketers, they're brilliant." And by promoting its own mutual funds, Donoghue says, Fidelity has promoted mutual funds in general. Its funds also happen to be "good performers."

True, Fidelity isn't penny-pinching like Vanguard, Donoghue conceded. But if a Vanguard money-market fund got into trouble, Vanguard might not have the deep pockets to bail out its shareholders— whereas, he claims, "Fidelity would not hesitate." His conclusion: "Cheap isn't necessarily better. *Better* is better."

Schabacker voted for T. Rowe Price: "They've put together funds that investors feel they need, from internationals to short-term globals. They're also very no-load oriented and provide good investor service." He also praised Vanguard and Fidelity, calling Fidelity "the biggest and the best. They give you the greatest choices, and a large percentage of them are simply outstanding."

Brouwer was the only panelist who voted for Harbor. He chose it because Owens-Illinois, which runs it and has its own pension money there, set the funds up "logically": It created a variety of categories with different risk-reward characteristics, then appointed good managers.

I voted for Fidelity, Vanguard, T. Rowe Price, Janus, and Neuberger & Berman. (While the questionnaire asked for only three choices, hey, it was *my* questionnaire.) Neuberger & Berman is a sterling family too often overlooked in polls like this, and the Janus funds are equally as classy. (Fittingly, Stanley Egener, president of Neuberger & Berman, is an admirer of Janus and has even suggested that investors buy both the value-oriented Neuberger & Berman funds and the growth-oriented Janus funds.)

CHAPTER 11

The Worst Families

Some families just have lots of children with positively atrocious records, the Steadman family being a chief offender in this regard. Other families of funds come with high sales charges and high fees. Still other families just don't offer well-rounded choices of individual funds.

To certain panelists, though, a family that they "don't admire" seems to be an otherwise fine family with a keenly disappointing flaw.

Asked to name the large mutual fund family that they "admired the least," in 1996 the panelists voted for these families (the number of nominations is in parentheses):

Steadman (5)

Keystone (4)

Scudder (2)

Dreyfus (2)

Dean Witter (2)

First Investors (2)

This time around, Stein voted for "brokerage house families."

There were single votes for American Heritage, Astra, Bull & Bear, Eaton Vance, Federated, Franklin, Gabelli, Lindner, Montgomery, Paine Weber, Pilgrim, and Stein Roe. It's startling that Gabelli, Lindner, Montgomery, and SteinRoe received nominations. It's astonishing that Scudder, the first no-load mutual fund and a family with a reputation for being "upright and God-fearing," received two votes.

In the previous poll, the least admired families were Fidelity (4), Dreyfus (2), Franklin (2), and Keystone (2). The animosity against Fidelity stemmed, in great part, from its seemingly high expenses. This time around, Fidelity received no negative votes. Franklin also dropped out of the higher echelons of the "Not Admired" list, no doubt because, in the meantime, it stopped assessing sales charges on reinvested distributions, a no-no that few other families were guilty of.

Keystone has soared almost to the top of the list. It was surpassed by Steadman only because, in the previous poll, panelists had been asked not to mention Steadman—a lapse on my part this time.

The Steadman funds have become a laughingstock. The four Steadman funds have compiled execrable records year after year because Charles Steadman buys the very worst of "story" stocks—stocks with no persuasive numbers but plenty of tall tales. The family has shut its funds to new investors—strange, considering how few new investors might choose them.

I voted for Dean Witter, Keystone, and First Investors—the last not just because of its funds' overall poor record but because of their intolerably high sales charges: 6.2% even on fixed-income funds. My resentment against Dean Witter may linger because it used to reward its brokers with higher commissions if they sold Dean Witter funds, a sinful practice that it has since renounced.

Other comments from the panelists on their unfavorite fund families:

Weber: "Steadman—you knew this was coming!"
Brouwer: "Too many."
Humphries: "Load families."

Stein's unfavorite (no-load) family was Dreyfus, which he claims doesn't offer enough good stock funds or international funds. He avoids its strategic funds because they come with sales charges.

Another critic of Dreyfus said: "They haven't made a significant effort on the equity side. They have not produced results ordinarily reflective of their size and maturity." Later that critic backpedaled, saying that he has become convinced that Dreyfus is trying to improve the performances of its stock funds.

Brouwer voted for Keystone: "It has the most onerous fee schedule, with 1.25% 12b-1 fees and everything else, along with spotty performances. It epitomizes the worst."

CHAPTER 12

The Best Load Funds

Load funds are those that carry sales charges. You buy such funds through stockbrokers or financial planners, not directly from the fund, and the commission you pay—up to 8.5%—helps pay the stockbroker or financial planner.

Obviously, load funds as a group simply will not do as well as no-load funds: Investors don't have all their money working for them.

For investors who aren't interested in managing their own money, because they don't have the interest, the skill, or the time, there's nothing inherently wrong with buying load funds. There are, indeed, estimable load funds—and wretched no-load funds. (Steadman is a no-load family.)

Besides, if you invest in stock funds with sales charges, intending to hold on for years, the commission you pay may not seem onerous compared with the long-term profit you should walk away with.

———

Asked to name the best load funds, the panelists gave two votes each to the American Funds in Los Angeles and to Morgan Stanley.

Says Phillips about Morgan Stanley: "It's the family that other load funds want to be like. It has a track record of conservative, wonderful results. It doesn't overpromise, and it doesn't try to shoot out all the lights. It doesn't have an aggressive growth fund, but it does have several different growth and income funds, and in the real world it's made money for its shareholders."

Skala says about American: "It's a conservative family, and fairly consistently does well. The funds tend not to move down much in a down market. It employs a team approach—a team, not a committee. Different managers manage some of the money."

Members of the American family are also somewhat diffident: "They don't toot their horns," Skala notes. "Only if you push and shove can you quote any of them. They're sort of 'Aw, shucks, folks.'"

Other load families that received single votes included Putnam and Franklin/Templeton.

SECTION III

ISSUES AND ANSWERS

CHAPTER 13

Traders versus Investors

"Traders" are people who flit in and out of the stock market and in and out of particular stocks. On Monday, they buy a stock at, say, $12.75; by Thursday, the stock is up to $13.50 (or down to $11.125), and the traders sell—and move on. Whether they made a lot or a little money, or lost a lot or a little money, depends on how many shares they bought in the first place.

At the opposite pole are "investors," people who buy a stock on Monday, then consider selling three years later. They claim that they're buying the company, not "playing the market"; some argue that, to determine whether a stock was a good buy or not, you must give it a full year. Others talk about "full market cycles," which might be three, four, or even more years. (A cycle includes a bull and a bear market.)

Investors have enjoyed the better press. "I've never met a trader who wound up making money" is a statement attributed to so many different people that it has probably entered the realm of folklore. The conventional wisdom, no matter what the subject, tends to be conservative—and "investing" is certainly more conservative than "trading."

A notable finding from the questionnaires I sent to mutual fund experts was that they, too, are divided along trader-investor lines. They, too, disagreed about whether shareholders should be opportunistic or be patient—whether they should flit around from fund to fund or stick with funds in which they have confidence.

Here's how the two types of people might be differentiated:

Opportunistic (traders)	**Patient** (investors)
Short-term oriented	Long-term oriented
Sprinter	Long-distance runner
Hare	Tortoise
Microscopic	Macroscopic

Some examples from the questionnaires:

Many of the panelists thought that a fund's one-year record was important to consider in evaluating a fund. Many others thought it was unimportant.

By the same token, many thought that a fund's 10-year record was important; just about the same number thought it was not important.

When should you sell a disappointing fund? Many panelists would sell a growth fund if it underperformed for a year. A somewhat higher number would be a little more patient, and wait more than a year.

In short, the panelists were almost evenly divided on whether they were traders or investors in mutual funds.

Market-timers presumably are more opportunistic than patient investors: That's part of the definition of market-timers, that they shift from declining markets, or markets about to decline, to thriving markets, or markets about to thrive. And, in general, panelists who would shift out of poor-performing funds quickly, and who stressed funds' short-term records, also considered themselves further advanced along the continuum of market-timers.

Merriman and Donoghue were the strongest self-identified timers; Phillips and Kolluri, the strongest buy-and-holders. Merriman and Donoghue both thought a fund's record for less than a year was very important; Kolluri and Phillips, unimportant. Merriman

CHAPTER 13 Traders versus Investors   121

and Donoghue might sell a poor-performing fund in less than a year; Kolluri and Phillips would give it more leeway.

But the correlation fell apart with regard to Berry and Weber, whose strategy is to move from top-performing fund to top-performing fund: Both consider themselves rather mild market-timers. (See Chapter 24 for more on market-timing.)

Skala is a rather patient investor: Where 1 is opportunistic and 5 patient, he rated himself a 4. He doesn't consider a fund's performance over less than a year significant: He emphasizes a fund's five-year record, then its 10-year record, then its three-year record, then its one-year record, and—finally—its record for less than a year. Before selling an underperforming fund, he would wait more than a year.

In response to the question, "Why do funds do well?" his answer: A consistent strategy. Not so important was willingness to be less aggressive in a bear market.

In measuring a fund's performance, Skala stresses its total return over the years, then its consistency of performance, performance in up and down markets, and performance vis-à-vis its peers.

Not surprisingly, to Skala a successful manager is patient. (He or she also has strong self-esteem, is intelligent, and is experienced.)

As a market-timer, Skala rated himself in the middle—between mild and strong.

Weber is an opportunistic investor, candidly saying that he's "biased" against buy-and-holders. "Look at the Japanese market," he argues. "The Japanese are at least as clever as we are. Yet in September of 1992, the Japanese market was down 62% from its high of 1989, at the same point as it was in 1986. And if it can happen there, it can happen here."

On the opportunist-patient continuum, Weber ranked himself a 2 (rather opportunistic). In evaluating funds, he emphasizes a one-year time period, then less than a year and three years. Naturally, he would sell poor-performing stock funds in less than a year. Still, he thinks that a key reason a fund does well year after year is that the manager is patient (along with being logical and experienced).

Another opportunistic investor was Donoghue, although he rated himself just a step below "patient." He will hold on to a fund as long as it does well, he explains. "But it's important to know when to say good-bye. Keeping your money is as important as making money. You can't keep your money in one sector and have a steadily growing portfolio."

Donoghue is a momentum-investor, like Berry and Weber. "We find that any performance record over one year is useless," he says. He ranks funds on a weighted average of one-, three-, six-, and 12-month performances.

He will sell a poor-performing fund after less than a year—and would definitely sell if the fund underperformed its peers and he couldn't determine why.

On the market-timing continuum, Donoghue places himself a step to the right of "absolute."

Pope was a little unusual. He has two portfolios, one that he calls his "core" portfolio—made up of funds with good 1-year records—and a portfolio of funds that he uses to have fun with. Typical core funds: Lindner Growth and Mutual Shares. Typical "crap-shooting" (as he calls them) funds: Fidelity Selects. He holds his core portfolio through thick and thin, his fun portfolio only through thick. So Pope imaginatively embraces both styles: patient and opportunistic.

CHAPTER 14

Open-Ends versus Closed-Ends

Shares of closed-end funds are bought and sold by the investors themselves on stock exchanges. The number of shares such a fund issues is limited.

With open-end funds, investors buy shares from the fund and sell shares to the fund, either directly or through brokers or financial planners.

One consequence of this difference is that the price per share of a closed-end fund may differ from its net asset value, depending on what shareholders are willing to pay. Sometimes investors may be willing to pay more than the shares are essentially worth: The shares sell at a premium. More often, they are willing to pay less than the shares are essentially worth: The shares are selling at a discount. (Stock funds are more likely to trade at a discount than fixed-income funds.)

With an open-end fund, shares trade at their net asset value: whatever the shares are inherently worth (plus any sales charge).

A chief benefit of closed-end funds is that if shareholders panic and sell their shares, the managers need not sell their holdings to meet redemptions, perhaps dumping excellent stocks at fire-sale prices. Instead, the prices of the fund's shares simply go down.

With an open-end fund, the managers may have to sell excellent stocks cheaply just to pay off fleeing shareholders.

A chief drawback of closed-ends is that investing in them can be tricky. The individual securities in a fund may rise in price, but the fund's price may decline. Or a fund's price may remain in the dumps for no apparent reason, while the managers of the fund stubbornly refuse to turn it into an open-end to realize the difference between the fund's low price and the generally higher prices of the fund's securities.

There's nothing wrong with owning shares of open-ends along with closed-ends. After all, if you buy shares of closed-ends when they are trading at an unusually high discount, you can be fairly assured of making a profit eventually.

The term "mutual funds" usually means open-end investment companies, not closed-ends, which are the strange Uncle Harrys of mutual funds. There are fewer of the closed-ends; they aren't as well publicized or as well understood.

Most of the panelists work exclusively with open-end funds, which helps explain why most prefer them. Another obvious reason most preferred open-ends is that many can be bought without the buyer paying commissions.

Two panelists who didn't prefer open-ends were William Droms, a professor of finance, and Don Phillips of Morningstar, which publishes literature about both closed-ends and open-ends.

Phillips argues that because closed-ends are neglected, there are bargains ("inefficiencies") that shrewd investors can take advantage of. The reason that closed-ends are neglected in the first place, he explains, is that stock investors prefer ordinary stocks—and mutual fund investors consider closed-ends to be too much like stocks (which is, of course, what they are).

Closed-ends are also appropriate for markets without much liquidity, such as those in South America, Phillips argues. If investors redeem their shares, the market won't be roiled as much.

Pope gave an interesting explanation for his preference for open-ends: He has conducted studies that show that a healthy cash flow helps the performance of an open-end fund. It's not because people throw money into a fund during a bull market, Pope maintains. Apparently it's because the manager can do better when he is fully invested. Or perhaps the manager just has a "hot hand." But with a closed-end fund, the managers don't benefit when more investors buy shares: The price just goes up, and the managers don't have extra cash to invest.

But Pope has become slightly dubious about this theory recently, when funds can become so gigantic.

Here are comments from the other panelists who preferred open-end funds:

"Ease of entry and exit at net asset value." —Kolluri

"If you buy a closed-end fund, you must deal with two sources of volatility: the people who trade the individual securities and the people who trade shares of the closed-end fund."— Higgins

"All of your initial investment goes to work for you."—Schabacker

"There's no need to worry about deviation between net asset value and price; you also have more choices of investment styles and objectives."—Skala

"Closed-end funds have market and NAV risk. Open-ends only have NAV risk. And IPO buyers in closed-end funds almost always lose."—Berry (New closed-ends typically sink to a discount when brokers stop trying to sell them to their customers.)

"Open-ends face the uncertainty of the stock market. Closed-ends have that same uncertainty, plus the uncertainty of how other investors will perceive the fund and its manager."—Weber

"Open-ends have liquidity, established value, and no or minimal trading costs."—Merriman

"There's a larger universe of open-end funds and fund strategies and managers to choose from. Closed-ends are a specialty item dependent on fluctuations in the premium. Also, many open-ends have no trading costs, unlike closed-ends."—Stein

"Closed-ends are generally less aggressive. Exception: Specialized funds such as single-country funds when open-ends are unavailable."—Jacobs

Open-ends have (1) Liquidity—Can buy or sell unlimited number of shares. Closed-end funds are frequently hard to buy or sell in any quantity. (2) No discounts/premiums—Can buy at NAV (no-load only)."—Brouwer

"I don't like to always pay commissions. And I believe cash flow helps a fund manager."—Pope

"(1) Ease of transactions (i.e., buying and selling); (2) more options available."—Litman

Even one of the two panelists who did not prefer open-ends to closed-ends, in his explanation, seemed to favor open-ends:

"I prefer closed-end funds for illiquid securities, especially when at a discount. Otherwise, open-end funds offer more advantages."—Phillips

Closed-Ends versus Open-Ends

Type	How to buy shares	Sales price	Shares outstanding
Open-end	Through fund or salesperson	Net asset value	Varies
Closed-end	Through salesperson	Market price	Limited

CHAPTER 15

Six Ways of Evaluating Funds

Oddly enough, it can be difficult to determine whether a fund has a good track record. Even the experts will disagree about even famous funds.

The first and simplest way to gauge a fund's performance is to track its total return over a specific time period—without regard to what kind of fund it is, stock or fixed income. This is the method used by Investor's Business Daily, and it is obviously flawed. A volatile aggressive-growth fund's performance shouldn't be measured against the performance of a stable short-term Treasury fund. This type of rating system penalizes stable, conservative funds.

Another way to evaluate funds is to compare the total returns of similar funds—aggressive-growth funds against other aggressive growth funds, for example.

But if you are guided only by a fund's total returns over the years, you would then be ignoring the fund's volatility. Do you really want to own shares of a fund that goes up 10% one year, down 5% the next year, up 15% the next, down 7% the following year? Wouldn't you prefer a fund that steadily rises year after year, if more modestly?

So, instead of looking at only a fund's total return, you might zero in on its consistency of performance—its steady appreciation year after year. That's a third gauge.

A sophisticated way of checking a fund's consistency is to penalize it for its volatility and reward it for its stability—to give it a "risk-adjusted" rating. That's what Morningstar, Inc., does, although Morningstar doesn't penalize funds for volatility on the way up. The Value Line Mutual Fund Survey also uses risk-adjusted ratings, but it *does* punish funds even for upside volatility.

But, as touchstones of performance, concentrating just on consistency and establishing risk-adjusted ratings have flaws, too. Exceedingly conservative funds can be rewarded excessively; aggressive funds can be punished severely.

Two examples: The Valley Forge Fund is conservative, perhaps too conservative. It's really a money-market fund that every so often makes a lightning-quick foray into an underpriced blue-chip stock, snatches a quick profit, then transforms itself into a placid money-market fund again. Morningstar loves its stability. It usually rates Valley Forge above average.

But Valley Forge's total return over the years has been anemic. The "No-Load Fund Investor" emphasizes a fund's total return, not its risk-adjusted return, and it puts Valley Forge in the bottom quintile of its supposed fund category, growth funds.

Twentieth Century Ultra is an exceedingly volatile fund, and Morningstar punishes it for its vagaries. Although the fund has a splendid total return over the years, Morningstar has rated it only slightly above average. The "No-Load Fund Investor" places it in the top quintile.

Recently I compared total-return ratings and risk-adjusted ratings for a variety of funds and found that they agreed only 62% of the time.

The risk-adjusted rating also has a glaring problem with entire categories of funds, namely high-yield, low-rated corporate bond and municipal bond funds. The riskiness inherent in these funds isn't reflected by their volatility. Volatility may be a kissing cousin of risk; it's not an identical twin.

So all four of these methods of evaluating funds seem to be imperfect—being guided by a fund's total return, its total return compared with its peers, and being guided by either its consistency or its risk-adjusted rating.

CHAPTER 15 Six Ways of Evaluating Funds   **129**

A fifth way: Instead of comparing a growth fund's performance against another growth fund's performance, you compare the performances against an index—typically, in the case of stocks, the S&P 500. What if all growth funds had soared in one year? What should a fund that appreciated by 10% be penalized, compared to one that appreciated by 15%, when the S&P 500 went up only 5%?

On the other hand, sometimes the indexes are inappropriate. A small-company fund's performance should be compared with the performance of an index of small companies, not the S&P 500—yet this is what typically happens. And balanced funds cannot easily be compared with any single index because such funds include both stocks and bonds—in varying percentages.

Jacobs insists that "99% of all comparisons of fund records to indexes are invalid. They're meaningless; they're nonsensical. I run two balanced portfolios, and how can they be compared with the S&P 500 when my portfolios are 35% in bonds? It's comparing apples to oranges."

A sixth way of evaluating funds is to investigate how creditably they performed during bull markets, how discreditably during bear markets. This is actually an indirect way of checking their volatility, but volatility only at (supposedly) the most vital time periods. Still, if a fund has a good total return and has acquitted itself with honor in both up markets and down markets, you have a combination of the total return and risk-adjustment measures.

The objection here is that funds that excel during bull and bear markets of the past may not excel during bull and bear markets of the future. *Forbes* uses this bull-and-bear approach in compiling its Honor Roll, and (a) its list of best funds often changes drastically from year to year, and (b) during the crash of 1987, its top funds, supposedly invulnerable to bear markets, performed just like all other funds.

Besides, as Phillips points out, there's not always agreement over exactly when a bear market or bull market has occurred. Perhaps examining a fund's volatility continuously and not just during certain periods—the risk-adjusted approach—is better. In fact, Phillips thinks that it's important to know how a fund has fared during "transitional" periods, between bull and bear markets.

Then, too, if you intend to hold a fund for a long period, you might be more concerned about how a fund performs in bull markets, not in bear markets. This is the same limitation of the general risk-adjusted approach: Despite its superb track record, Twentieth Century Ultra never makes the Forbes' Honor Roll.

Higgins argues that how a fund fares in up and down markets is important, but he prefers risk-adjusted returns in general, "so that data merely substantiate other data."

Clearly, in evaluating funds, an investor should check various gauges of its past performance, not just one. Another obvious conclusion: The total-return method is best for aggressive investors, the risk-adjusted method for conservative investors.

The question for the panelists was: Which are the best ways to measure a fund's performance?

The panelists considered a fund's performance vis-à-vis its peers the single best way to gauge a fund's performance.

Next (in importance): A fund's consistency of performance.

Third: Its total return over the years.

Fourth: Its performance in up and in down markets.

Fifth: Its performance vis-à-vis an appropriate index.

Sixth: Its performance vis-à-vis its volatility.

Savage doesn't seem especially upset about a fund's volatility: "It's not that I'm not bothered by it. But for a long-term investor, there are two ways that volatility can work to your advantage. One, you can buy different types of volatile funds so that, collectively, they are not as volatile individually; and two, you are rewarded by taking on that risk. People tend to overstate the risk. The risk of losing money in the market is much greater over a one-year period and much, much lower over a longer period."

Brouwer stresses how well a fund did during clear-cut bull and bear markets. "How badly was it hit in October of 1987? How long did it take to get back to where it was?" He also focuses on how a fund has performed in comparison with its peers.

Higgins, Jacobs, and Weber stressed performance vis-à-vis peers; Litman, that plus total return over the years plus consistency; Donoghue emphasized only performance vis-à-vis peers plus consistency.

Schabacker paid the most attention to performance vis-à-vis peers plus performance in both up and down markets.

Droms placed equal weight on all six measures; so did Berry, except he denigrated performance vis-à-vis volatility. Pope focused on performance vis-à-vis peers, in both up and down markets, total return over the years, and consistency of performance.

I myself would emphasize performance vis-à-vis peers plus vis-à-vis volatility.

Phillips zeroed in on total return and consistency.

The upshot seems to be that, in judging a fund, you must use art as well as science. You must weigh the various ways you can evaluate a fund, figure out what you want from that fund, and decide which criteria are most appropriate.

If you have a long-term investment horizon and are seeking maximum capital gains, your gauges of a fund's past performance would likely be different from those of someone with a short-term investment horizon, someone willing to sacrifice breathtaking gains for stability.

Six Gauges of Fund Performance

1. Total return over the years.
2. Total return compared with its peers.
3. Steady, consistent appreciation year after year.
4. Total return compared with an appropriate index.
5. Total return compared with volatility of price.
6. Performance in bull markets and bear markets.

CHAPTER 16

Which Time Period to Stress?

Before buying shares of a fund, you will of course check its past performance. But there's a tricky question: Over what period of time? Six months? Ten years?

Here are the time periods the panelists stressed during an earlier poll of 17 people:

1. Less than a year: Seven voted for 1, two for 2, two for 3, one for 4, four for 5. (1 was "most important.")
2. Five years: Six voted for 1, three for 2, three for 3, two for 4, three for 5.
3. One year: Five voted for 1, six for 2, two for 3, three for 4, one for for 5.
4. Three years: Three voted for 1, five for for 2, five for for 3, two for for 4, two for for 5.
5. Ten years or longer (the questionnaire specified that panelists assume that the manager has not changed): Three voted for for 1, two for for 2, three for for 3, four for for 4, five for for 5.
6. All periods: One voted for 1, six for 2, four for 3, four for 5.

Here is the ranking according to votes for 1s plus 2s and 4s plus 5s:

1. Five years (10 high, 5 low)
2. Three years (6 high, 3 low)
3. Less than a year (8 high, 7 low)
4. One year (8 high, 7 low)
5. Ten years (7 high, 9 low)
6. All periods (4 high, 4 low)

Jacobs stressed the records of less than a year, one year, three years, and five years, but not ten years. "There's empirical evidence, including some research I've done, that shows that ten-year records aren't good forecasters," he relates, "whereas time periods of up to five years are good forecasters." He also notes that over ten years the original manager may have left—and the fund's size may have changed. If it was a small fund eight to ten years ago, it may be a large fund now, and thus a different kettle of fish. In fact, Jacobs points out, a fund's earlier years may have produced the healthy total returns that overcome a fund's recent sorry performance.

Pope voted for both less than one year and for ten years, his strategy being to divide his holdings into a core section and into a crap-shooting section. With the core holdings, he looks at long-term records; with the gambling holdings, short-term records. "Sometimes I'm upset that Lindner or Mutual Shares don't participate fully in a bull market," he says, "but then I take a look at the long-term charts and see how well they performed in bear markets."

In evaluating funds, Stein preferred short time periods to five- and ten-year periods—even though he placed himself in the middle between opportunistic and patient investors. "There are so many new funds, and if you concentrate on five-year records, you eliminate a lot of newer funds," he explains. "If you just look at a couple of years, you have enough ups and downs to get a reading on a fund, to get a sense of how volatile it is, how it does in up markets and in down markets."

Savage doesn't especially value a three-year time period: "Three years tends to be about the length of the typical market cycle. But it makes more sense to evaluate a fund over a longer time

CHAPTER 16 Which Time Period to Stress?

period." If you buy a utilities fund for its three-year performance, he says, very likely its run has ended.

Markman emphasizes one- and three-year periods in choosing funds. "I think that the nature of the financial market has changed so much. What it did during 1987 or 1988, what it did 10 years ago, is not necessarily relevant to how it's going to react to the environment today." Also, the growth of funds over the last 10 years has been so vast that concentrating on longer time periods "would eliminate from consideration 60% or 65% of the funds that are out there."

"I choose funds more on the manager than on the three- versus five-year record," says Henrietta Humphries. "But other things being equal, I incline slightly toward the three-year record."

Still, the disagreements over which time periods to emphasize stem mainly from the fact that the panelists were divided into the opportunistic and the patient.

Here's how the eight patient investors rated the time periods:

1. Five years (7 high, 0 low)
2. Three years (5 high, 1 low)
3. Ten years (3 high, 3 low)
4. One year (3 high, 4 low)
5. All periods (3 high, 1 low; only 4 ballots)
6. Less than a year (2 high, 5 low)

For most investors, who no doubt consider themselves patient investors, the time periods to emphasize in evaluating a fund's performance seem to be five years and three years, then ten years and one year.

The one investor who designated himself as a complete opportunist, Paul Merriman, predictably gave less-than-one-year a 1, one year a 3, three years a 5, five years a 5, and ten years a 5.

CHAPTER 17

The Worst Handicaps

With at least 33 very attractive funds out there, how does one narrow them down into one concise portfolio? Our panelists, after all, generally believe that five to eight funds are all that someone needs.

One answer is to eliminate funds with handicaps. A handicap is any extra weight, any flaw, anything at all that may tend to drag down a fund's performance in the future. Let's say that you must choose between two funds with similar superb performance records. If one fund has only a two-year record, while the other has a five-year record, there's your answer. You would choose the fund with the longer record. Other things being equal, the manager—assuming the same person has remained at the helm—has had more experience, and his fund has been tested over a longer period of time. In a fund, newness is a handicap.

The questionnaire asked the panelists to rank the importance of a variety of handicaps. Here is the order in which the handicaps wound up:

Worst Handicaps (1 out of 5)
- High volatility not matched by results (13 gave it a 1, two a 2, one a 3, one a 5)

- High front-end load (12 gave it a 1, three a 2, one a 3, one a 4)
- Lack of a clear strategy (11 gave it a 1, three a 2, one a 3, one a 5)
- Deferred sales charge (10 gave it a 1, three a 2, one a 3, two a 4)

Serious Handicaps (2 out of 5)
- High 12b-1 fee (over 0.25%) (four gave it a 1, seven a 2, four a 3) (A 12b-1 fee is a charge for marketing expenses—a "hidden load.")
- Newness (seven gave it a 2, four a 3, three a 4, two a 5)

Definite Handicap (3 out of 5)
- High volatility (one gave it a 1, three a 2, eight a 3, four a 4, one a 5)

Less Important
- Giant size (one gave it a 1, one a 2, 11 a 3, three a 4)

Jacobs doesn't worry much about a fund with a high turnover (the fund buys and sells frequently), claiming that most studies have shown no correlation between a high turnover and poor overall performance. Still, he concedes, a high turnover may mean you have a higher tax bill—unless your fund is in your tax-sheltered account.

Similarly, Stein said that he pays less attention to a stock fund's expenses, to its turnover, and to its 12b-1 fees than to its results: "I'm bottom-line oriented." With fixed-income funds, where margins may not be so high, he's more concerned with expenses. With stock funds, he simply avoids front-end and (undiminishing) back-end loads.

Schabacker didn't consider low front-end loads "a major headache," and thought that even a high front-end load is tolerable if you plan to hold a well-performing fund for 10 years. As for a high turnover, he rather likes it: "If the manager achieves a good performance with a high turnover, that's fine with me. He's a fast mover. And if I have the fund in a pension plan, I don't have to worry about capital gains." A high turnover with a mediocre performance, he stipulated, is a totally different kettle of fish.

CHAPTER 17 The Worst Handicaps 139

Skala did not view volatility as excessively worrisome, noting that investors intimidated by volatility "could very well never own 20th Century funds and, over 10 years, be very sorry." (The 20th Century funds are momentum-oriented and remain fully invested; while their volatility tends to be high, their returns tend to match.)

Volatility is acceptable in a fund, Skala argues, if you have a fairly long time-horizon and can wait out any declines—and the fund has a history of good returns.

Weber expressed the same view: "There are plenty of examples of volatile funds that do well. The 20th Century funds fluctuate greatly, but their long-term record remains above average. They always end up at the top over three- and four-year cycles."

Jacobs agreed: "If you have a long-term horizon, volatility shouldn't be intimidating. But if you have a short-term horizon, you should be concerned." (Earlier he had quipped, "I'm not concerned about volatility . . . unless it happens to *me*.")

As a momentum-follower, Donoghue naturally doesn't regard volatility as a handicap: "Volatility is opportunity. It's not risk."

Markman doesn't like a high front-end load, but a high turnover doesn't necessarily faze him: "A front-end load is an expense that doesn't relate to the manager's job. A load never creates value. But a high turnover can create value in the portfolio—it's not a guarantee, but it's not a definite loss." A high turnover, of course, can mean that the manager is selling companies that are cooling and buying companies that are heating up.

Endorsing funds that have clear strategies, says Schabacker, is like being in favor of motherhood. Still, some funds seem opportunistic, moving from undervalued stocks to growth stocks. "And as an investor," he argues, "if you're not sure what your strategy is, you're going to wind up a loser."

Pope avoids funds without clear strategies. For example, some income funds, he complains, seem to have an unnatural supply of growth stocks, as do some growth and income funds.

Stein also was dubious of funds without clear strategies. The clearer a fund's game plan, the more likely he is to put money into it.

Phillips recalls talking to one portfolio manager who was value-oriented early in 1987, mentioning Ben Graham and his criteria for identifying bargain stocks. As the year went along and the manager's fund slipped behind because of his huge cash position, he decided that it wasn't undervalued stocks that he wanted to own so much as it was relatively undervalued stocks—"even if they are expensive." Later in the year, he was so uncertain what to do that he was waiting for the elves on "Wall Street Week" to guide him. "I knew he was confused then," says Phillips.

It's not easy to stick by your strategy, Phillips admits, especially when other managers are doing better than you are and you begin to wonder whether you should emulate them to at least a small extent—at which point "you begin losing your identity."

Brouwer mentions "fuzzy" funds as those to avoid, those that "do whatever seems hot, whether in stocks or bonds." One famous fund, he goes on, boasts in its prospectus that it does top-down and bottom-up investing, consulting with analysts around the world who embrace a variety of investing styles. "The fund uses every investment strategy known to man," Brouwer says scornfully, "but it still doesn't have a style."

Donoghue agrees that an unclear strategy is a major handicap of mutual funds—and notes that if a fund simply proclaims that it invests in growth stocks, its strategy can still be unclear.

Stein is a bit skeptical of new funds: "You want to see some track record. New funds can be hyped. They may have administrative problems. And someone with a wonderful record elsewhere may not do well right away. So I'd rather give a fund a little time."

On the other hand, "I like new funds," says Brouwer. Ideally, the manager of a new fund has established a good track record somewhere else. The manager of a small fund, he argues, must work hard to set a good record for a few years. So the manager normally gives it his best ideas, along with much of his time and attention. "When it gets big and fat," Brouwer says, "the manager may be too busy giving interviews and involved in administrative details. He may be distracted."

Brouwer boasts that he bought shares of both Harbor International and Robertson Stephens Emerging Growth when they were new and small.

Litman also likes new funds, especially where the manager has a good long-term record elsewhere. Because the public probably isn't aware of the record, the fund won't quickly get top-heavy with money. "The average investor says, 'I never invest in a new fund,'" he says. "Actually, I suspect that new funds tend to do better." When Mario Gabelli started his funds a few years ago, the typical investor

CHAPTER 17 The Worst Handicaps

didn't know about his record managing private money, Littman points out. And his funds did better when they were smaller.

I myself like new funds created by families with good track records. Fidelity's new funds happen to have impressive records; apparently other Fidelity managers generously give tip-top ideas to these new managers. Besides, a new fund has a clean slate, and the manager can be exceedingly choosy about what he or she buys.

For the pros and cons of a large-sized fund, see the next chapter.

CHAPTER 18

Is Giant Size a Giant Handicap?

While the panelists weren't asked to define a "giant" fund, they would probably agree that a fund with $100 million in assets, or less, is small. If it's a fund that invests in small-company stocks, over $200 million may be large. Once a fund has over $500 million, it's surely getting large. At $1 billion and above, one is certainly in the land of the giants.

At one time, giant size was considered a gigantic impediment to a fund's performance. After all, a large fund cannot shift positions quickly without pushing stocks up or driving them down. The manager of one large Fidelity fund has reported that it takes him 75 days to load up on a new stock, or unload existing shares, without unduly affecting the prices.

Besides, a large fund cannot share much in the prosperity of small-company stocks. There aren't that many shares of a small-company stock available; even if a giant fund is locked in an enormous position, it wouldn't have much effect on the fund's subsequent performance.

These drawbacks are inarguable. Yet they aren't insuperable, as Peter Lynch proved while managing the Brobdingnagian Magellan Fund. The fact is that giant funds have advantages, too.

The 17 panelists in the earlier poll were asked to weigh the various possible advantages of a fund's being large. Here's how these advantages were ranked:

1. Money and prestige to attract and keep good managers (13 considered this important, 4 not important).

    Voting with the minority was Littman, who argues that many good managers prefer running their own ships: "They're independent thinkers and prefer being independent in general. So the big bucks that the big funds can offer them may not be enough to lure them away, or keep them."

2. Money and prestige to attract and keep good analysts (12 important, 5 not important).

3. Managers can learn from other managers in a family (11 important, 5 unimportant).

4. They are not so affected by shareholder buying and selling (10 important, 7 not important).

    Jacobs doubts that this is true. While some small funds have one or two large shareholders whose sudden departure could cause havoc, he believes, other small funds have many small accounts and thus are protected against sudden, severe shocks.

    Besides, even large funds can take pretty big hits: Fidelity Magellan, Jacobs points out, lost $1 billion in the crash of 1987.

    Phillips also had trouble with the notion that larger funds have more modest problems with redemptions. Large funds have high visibility, he points out, and this might translate into powerful waves of redemptions in bad times. Still, he granted that small funds can be severely injured if a few large shareholders pull out.

5. They receive more tips from good outside analysts (9 important, 8 unimportant).

    Litman was dubious: "Some analysts are just pushing a stock. No doubt some tips are good, but I don't think there's a direct correlation between the number of tips a fund gets and its quality."

CHAPTER 18 Is Giant Size a Giant Handicap?   145

    Phillips was similarly dubious. Even a relatively small fund like FPA Paramount gets plenty of phone calls, he notes, because the portfolio manager, William Sams, is known to act promptly on suggestions.

6. They enjoy economies of scale (7 important, 8 unimportant).

    Weber, who checked "unimportant," pointed to evidence that large funds don't necessarily pass along their lower expenses to shareholders. And Schabacker thought that once a fund gets beyond a certain size, "There's not a lot of correlation between size and fees."

    Brouwer agreed. With exceptions like Vanguard and PIMCO, large funds "keep what they save." He pointed out that Fidelity Magellan, the largest stock mutual fund, has a rather high expense ratio, 1%.

    Higgins concedes that economies of scale are important for fixed-income funds and equity-income funds, but "the bottom line with equity funds is a heavy dose of high return."

7. Large funds must tilt toward biggest stocks (5 important, 11 unimportant).

    The rationale for this supposed advantage was that (a) big-company stocks by and large did exceptionally well in the 1980s, whereas small-company stocks by and large did poorly, and (b) generally, a fund that buys big solid companies won't lead its shareholders to the slaughterhouse. Still, most panelists felt that a large fund's inability to profit much from small companies was a drawback, not an advantage.

CHAPTER 19

When to Sell

Opportunistic investors sell far more readily than patient investors, but few investors buy and hold indefinitely. Obviously, stocks should be sold—ideally—just before signs of trouble appear: A key company executive leaves, a competitor makes a breakthrough, it becomes evident that someone has been cooking the books, an enormous liability case looms, or almost everybody simply wises up that the stock is overvalued. You might consider selling a fund for similar good reasons.

Or for more mundane reasons:

- You own shares of a growth stock and need more income.
- You need money—to buy a house, to start a new business, etc.
- You want to buy shares of a mutual fund you think will do better.

The panelists disagreed strongly on the best reasons to sell a fund. Here's how they voted on various reasons (sometimes fewer than 19 panelists cast ballots):

1. The fund deviates from its strategy without a clear reason:

Sell	Maybe	Hold
11	5	0

    Comments: The presumption is that the fund has not been doing well, and the manager has abandoned his discipline in hope of catching a new wave. But the conventional wisdom is that managers should stick to what they know—the discipline that made the fund successful in the first place.

    As Skala puts it, "A good manager should know himself. He shouldn't be a fad investor, skipping from style to style. He shouldn't presume that he can adopt a different investment approach. He should stay with the style that he knows best."

    Brouwer would also sell. As he explains, you buy a fund for a reason: It's good at buying small-company stocks, for example. If it changes course and buys blue chips instead, your reason for buying it has flown away.

    Berry wouldn't budge. So long as the fund continues to do well, he will hang on. Perhaps the manager has a good reason to abandon his strategy—to move from small-company stocks to big-company stocks, for example. Only when the manager begins to be proved wrong would Berry depart.

2. The fund falters and you cannot determine why:

Sell	Maybe	Hold
11	4	1

    Comments: Jacobs cast his ballot for "maybe." Perhaps the manager has just suffered a streak of bad luck: Stocks he bought declined for reasons no one could have guessed beforehand. "I might hold on until I determined what caused the poor performance," he says.

    Stein also voted maybe: "I look at it on a case-by-case basis," he explains.

    Brouwer also cast his ballot for maybe: If he's confident about a fund, he may hang on for six months or over a year. "Typically, when you sell a fund, or a stock, after a period of poor performance," he says sorrowfully, "you learn later that you sold at the very bottom."

3. Poor performance in that sector:

Sell	Maybe	Hold
9	6	1

Comments: Weber interpreted the question to mean a poor performance compared to similar funds with similar goals. (The question, as worded, was ambiguous.)

4. If the successful manager left a small family:

Sell	Maybe	Hold
7	8	1

Comments: Jacobs might sell his shares, whereas he probably wouldn't sell if the family were large. "Large families can come up with replacements easier," he believes. "There are 10 or 15 manager changes at Fidelity every year, and you don't see any decline in the performances. Fidelity has a farm team of bright young people. Small families usually don't have all that talent."

Litman would say bye-bye—unless the replacement had a good, verifiable track record. "It's a brand-new ball game," he says. "The question comes down to: Would I have bought the fund if the new manager had been the manager? After all, usually there are other pretty good funds out there."

5. If the successful manager left a large family:

Sell	Maybe	Hold
2	11	3

Comments: As Jacobs observes, there's evidence that large families have deep benches. After Peter Lynch left Fidelity Magellan, his successors—Morris Smith, Jeff Vinik—acquitted themselves well. Less publicized substitutions were put into effect gradually at Janus, Janus 20, Lindner Growth, and Lindner Dividend.

Donoghue, who might sell if the manager of a small family moved on, wouldn't sell if the manager of a large fund left. "It takes forever to change a large fund," he argues. "It's like trying to turn around an oceanliner as opposed to a speedboat."

Berry, of course, wouldn't sell a fund merely because the successful manager leaves. "When Peter Lynch left Fidelity Magellan," he recalls, "a lot of people called me and asked whether they should get out. I said do nothing—and they did damn well. What makes a fund successful is a strategy that works. And it will work if another manager takes over. There are a lot of darn good funds out there, and no one has heard of their managers."

"When a successful manager leaves," he says in summary, "it's a nonevent."

Pope's view: "It makes me uneasy when a manager leaves one of my core funds. I worry that the new manager will make great changes."

My own feeling: I would be more likely to remain with a large-family fund whose manager left than a small-family fund. But I would be inclined to leave in any case, so long as I wouldn't expose myself to large capital-gains taxes.

How long would you give a poor-performing fund before booting it out of your portfolio?

Litman might keep a poor-performing fund for over a year, figuring that the manager's style of investing may be temporarily out of fashion. But if the manager has new responsibilities and is superintending new funds now, and might be "wearing thin," Littman would consider leaving.

Jacobs might keep laggard growth funds, balanced funds, and fixed-income funds for more than a year before selling them. But not aggressive growth funds: With them he's impatient because "You can get hurt more."

Humphries wouldn't sell if a fund has lagged in line with its peer group: "I'd do some research, and if all the reasons for buying it were still there, I'd hold on."

Savage also doesn't want to play follow the leader: "If a fund is remaining consistent, a lot of times you can fall into the trap where you sell in favor of a better performer. Then the market shifts and the new one starts to lag. It's very tough to tell what's an anomaly and what's a more fundamental problem. Every time the market zigs, you zag. Every time the market zags, you zig. But you don't want to wait too long, because poor performance can persist. So wait at least a year, but not too much longer."

Skala might hold funds for more than a year, although he, too, might give an aggressive-growth fund less string. "Cycles in investing may go against you for more than a year," he reasons. "Some excellent funds may remain in the doldrums for several years—like Pennsylvania Mutual." In short, "I don't have a switch list. You can be too quick to pull the trigger. In 1991, many value funds did poorly; in 1992, many came back strongly."

Pope would keep fixed-income funds for longer than a year, simply because of their general stability. Besides, if a bond fund underperforms, typically it's not a steep nosedive consuming lots of money.

Weber feels the same way. He invests in Vanguard High Yield Bond, he says, because although its yield is the lowest of the junk-bond funds, it's also the safest: The quality of its bonds is unusually high. So he expects it to underperform other junk-bond funds in a typical year.

Here's the breakdown on how long the panelists would keep poor-performing funds:

Growth stock fund: Less than a year, 9; more than a year, 8.

Aggressive growth fund: Less than a year, 11; more than a year, 6.

Stock and bond (balanced) fund: Less than a year, 8; more than a year, 9.

Fixed-income fund: Less than a year, 8; more than a year, 9.

The time periods tallied with whether the panelists were distinctively opportunistic or patient.

Of seven self-styled patient investors, five (Phillips, Kolluri, Littman, Skala, and Brouwer) might keep all four types of funds for over a year; Droms might keep three of the four (not aggressive growth) for over a year; only Schabacker might hold on for less than a year. (Asked about this, Schabacker said that "It's wrong never to admit that you've made a mistake and just to hold on—especially if you're not talking about an all-weather fund.")

Of four self-styled opportunistic investors, three might sell all four funds in less than a year (Merriman, Higgins, Berry). Weber might sell three of the four—not the fixed-income fund.

My own decision on when to sell would depend on (1) whether I had a significant tax loss, and (2) how serious the underperformance was. With any sizable, deductible tax loss, I would probably sell the fund and—if similar funds also were in the dumps—move into a similar fund. If the loss wasn't deductible—because the fund was in my pension plan—I would be even quicker to pull the trigger. If a fund lost me only a modest amount of money, and all its peers were also behaving badly if not worse, I would hang tough—I hope—unless I thought the market itself was preparing to take a steep plunge.

CHAPTER 20

Why Some Funds Do Better Than Others

If we knew why one fund does better than another, why (for example) one fund that searches for undervalued stocks does better than another fund that also specializes in undervalued stocks, we would be closer to being able to determine which funds to buy.

Some answers are obvious. A fund with good analysts will fare better. Its analysts will talk to more people, read more trade journals, look at the numbers more carefully, and study the historical record more thoroughly.

But what about other explanations? Here is how they were rated on an earlier questionnaire:

1. The fund's strategy is consistent.
   Ten panelists voted this the most important reason; three ranked it second; three ranked it third; one ranked it fifth and last.
2. Shrewdness of the manager.
   Nine voted this most important; three gave it a 2; three gave it a 3; two gave it a 4.
3. Excellence of research.
   Seven panelists considered this most important. Eight voted it second; three voted it third.

4. The manager's personality.
   This was denigrated by many of the panelists: It received two first-place votes, two second-place, five third-place, one fourth-place, and seven votes for fifth-place (least important).
5. Luck.
   This possibility didn't fly. Two panelists gave it a 3, nine gave it a 4, and six gave it a 5. Markman was an exception (see below).

A second time around, at the suggestion of the panelists, two new possibilities were added: "style of investing" and "willingness to be less aggressive in a bear market."

The first implies that a fund that employs a particular strategy—say, looking for undervalued large stocks—may be less vulnerable than a fund that uses a more unusual strategy, or a more risky strategy, such as looking for small-company stocks on a tear.

The second explanation implies that the fund's managers employ at least a mild version of market-timing. Just before October 19, 1987, for example, the managers might not have been fully invested.

Here's how the explanations for exceptional fund performance fared on a second questionnaire:

1. Shrewdness of the manager.
   12 for 1, 2 for 2, 2 for 3, 1 for 4.
2. Consistency of strategy.
   7 for 1, 9 for 2, 1 for 3.
3. Style of investing.
   7 for 1, 6 for 2, 4 for 4.
4. Excellent research.
   6 for 1, 10 for 2, 1 for 3.
5. Willing to be less aggressive.
   4 for 1, 8 for 2, 3 for 3, 1 for 4, 1 for 5. Not surprisingly, opportunists thought this explanation was important; patient investors did not. Thus, Berry and Donoghue favored this as an explanation; Skala did not.

Higgins thinks a good manager accommodates his or her strategy to the realities, but within limits: "Never changing how you

CHAPTER 20 Why Some Funds Do Better Than Others

invest may not breed salutary results. You should concede to temporary pressures in declining markets. But this doesn't mean that the manager should abandon his strategy entirely."

Merriman stresses excellent research as an explanation of outstanding fund performance: With large-cap stocks, he maintains, the market is fairly efficient. The funds that do exceptionally well tend to concentrate not on the blue chips but on more thinly capitalized companies, which fewer analysts follow and where a fund's own research is important. "If 3M introduces a new product," Merriman says, "it will have nowhere near the effect that a new product would have on a small company, and it's up to the analyst to predict the success or failure of a small company's new product."

Phillips concurred in appreciating the value of research: "Success in this business doesn't come from trying to answer the big questions—where will the Dow be at the end of the year? Where are interest rates going?—but from answering questions like, Does this company have an advantage over its competitors? Investors make money by knowing something that others don't know, or seeing the significance of something that others don't."

Donoghue considered excellent research important, but not as important as a manager's willingness to go to cash in a bear market, or a manager's style of investing, consistency, and shrewdness. His argument: The manager of a Treasury fund, for example, doesn't need outstanding research.

Jacobs is somewhat dubious about the value of a fund manager's being "consistent." Says he, "No funds are terribly consistent. Yet the advice is given out so casually—'Look for consistency.' It's easy to say, hard to follow."

Savage also doesn't think that "consistency of strategy" explains why funds do well regularly: "It's very rare to find a strategy that will lead to outperformance year after year. The guy who's going to have a number of years in which he's better than average is going to jump from style to style." The question is whether someone will be able to maintain superior flexibility.

Markman thinks luck is important: "The markets are so complex. Speaking only for myself, my ability to grasp what's going on is so limited . . . If I were just relying on my brains, I wouldn't be doing nearly as well as I have. It's like talking to a professional athlete. A .300 batter is a .350 batter because of luck. There is only so much where skill will take you, but you can create an environment in which skill will take you to luck."

In general, the consensus was that a fund that does well year after year employs a shrewd manager, one who follows a strategy consistently, a strategy that is sensible and nicely balances risk and reward. Apparently the fund's manager and the fund's strategy are of comparable importance.

CHAPTER 21

Why Some Managers Do Better Than Others

Surely portfolio managers who have good records don't all come from the exact same mold. A value investor may be a different sort of person from a growth investor, for example—more patient, more relaxed, more Type B than Type A. The manager of sedate Valley Forge is probably a very different sort from the manager of a volatile fund such as PBHG Emerging Growth.

Still, it's possible that successful managers share some things in common, that Michael Price and Jean-Marie Eveillard and Mario Gabelli are brothers under the skin.

The panelists were asked to assess how important various attributes of successful managers are. The number of panelists that thought the following attributes were important is listed below:

Flexibility*	11
Experience	11
Coolness	8
Decisiveness	8
Independence of thought	8
Intelligence	7

---

* Defined in the questionnaire as willingness to change course in the face of new evidence.

Patience	7
Logic	5
Consistency	5
Passion for the business	5
Strong self-esteem	2

The 17 earlier panelists had been asked to rate, from 1 to 5, various aspects of a successful manager's personality.

Many different attributes received a median vote of 2 (just below most important): coolness, patience, strong self-esteem, flexibility, intelligence, logic, decisiveness, experience, and consistency. Only luckiness received a median vote of 4, or next to unimportant.

Still, more of the panelists gave 1 (the highest score) to these attributes: intelligence, decisiveness, and experience (8); patience and logic (7); consistency (6); coolness (5); and flexibility (4).

Flexibility went from 4 first-place nominations on the first round to 11 on the second—but only the second questionnaire defined flexibility. Coolness and strong self-esteem received two votes for 5.

Overall, the panelists apparently believe that successful managers are experienced and flexible—and perhaps independent thinkers, decisive, and cool as well.

Some panelists disagreed. Berry focuses almost exclusively on a fund's recent performance: "We don't pay much attention to the managers, only to the bottom line. We don't care whether one person is running the fund, as at Lindner, or an entire committee, as at some Fidelity funds."

The manager, Berry believes, is not so important as his strategy—whether he invests in growth stocks, value stocks, small-company stocks, or big-company stocks. That's why, according to Berry, a successful manager can leave a fund—and suddenly lose his touch at another fund. The leadership has changed: Growth stocks may have superseded value stocks; big-company stocks superseded small-company stocks. It's not the manager who has faltered. Change is the warp and woof of investing.

Weber emphasizes a successful manager's "shrewdness." Still, his view is that "If you take 100 managers, you may have one hundred very different personalities. There'll be shrewd managers;

CHAPTER 21 Why Some Managers Do Better Than Others

there'll be tenacious managers. A small number will be lucky. To me, results are first and foremost."

A manager's experience is "helpful," Weber goes on, especially if he or she has gone through bear markets along with bull markets. "Fidelity sometimes hires kids right out of college," he complains, "and while some of them do well, some don't."

Schabacker emphasizes the value of a manager's having a "formula that he's tried out and keeps testing—not going from one whim to another."

Jacobs thinks that one key aspect of a successful manager's personality is his ability to analyze large amounts of data. A touch of contrarianism, he believes, also helps.

Phillips mentions patience—and "a certain courage to behave differently. It's difficult to be different, but that's how you beat the market."

Brouwer thinks that investing is still "a lot more art than science," but believes that good managers are intelligent, logical, flexible, disciplined, and independent-thinking: "That's why Hakan Castegren at Harbor International is so good. He makes the decisions—a committee doesn't make them. So, when everyone else was buying Mexican stocks recently, for example, he was selling. And like other good managers, he also has a passion for the business."

Another quality that the best managers have, Brouwer suggests, is the ability to pull the trigger—to act decisively, even if they don't have all the facts. "Some managers wait for complete enlightenment," he claims. "They buy stocks that go up, then can't sell them, and wind up riding them back down. Good managers don't do that—they sometimes bank on their instincts."

Stein admits that "I haven't a clue as to how successful managers do it. All those adjectives—decisive, logical, flexible, cool, patient—help, no doubt. But someone's personality doesn't persuade me to invest. You can get fooled by personalities."

Having myself interviewed around 200 managers, I would say that the typical successful manager is smart . . . hard-working . . . quick-thinking . . . and independent-thinking. That he or she can buck the conventional view is consistent with high self-esteem (which may, of course, be accompanied by low self-esteem, which drives people like Peter Lynch to excel). I would also say that luck plays some part in success.

Merriman emphasizes the importance of a manager's being patient and consistent—as a market-timer, his own strategy requires patience and consistency, even when he seems to be missing a bull market or is trapped in a bear market.

Savage doesn't believe high self-esteem, or flexibility, is that important, but he does emphasize shrewdness: "Self-esteem is something that I have trouble relating to money management. I don't mind flexibility, but it suggests the possibility of inconsistency. Shrewdness suggests the ability to find opportunity."

Skala doesn't think that "logic" is a key element in a successful manager's personality. "The market is irrational," he insists, "not logical." Successful managers concentrate not just on economic and monetary measures, but on investor psychology as well. It's because the market can be so irrational, Skala argues, that "economists would be disasters as money managers." Skala voted for patience, flexibility, decisiveness, experience, and independence of thought as the cardinal qualities of top managers.

CHAPTER

Assembling an Entire Portfolio

The trouble with having just one or two funds is that the fund managers—and you—may be unlucky, even if only temporarily.

A manager's style—say, investing in seemingly undervalued large-company stocks—may fall out of favor. (There's a saying among mutual fund managers: Every fund is entitled to one bad year.) Or managers may lose their cool. If growth stocks aren't doing well, the manager may switch to undervalued stocks—just at the wrong time.

At the other extreme, an investor may have too many funds. There's safety in numbers, of course; but there's also mediocrity in numbers.

So, how many funds should you own? Five to eight was the consensus of the panelists. Seven chose 5 to 8; four chose 8 to 12; three chose 1 to 5; one chose 12 to 15; and one chose 15 or more.

A typical point of view was expressed by Ken Weber, who favors having just four or five funds: Beyond that, he believes, you're probably going to do only as well as the market because your portfolio will have so many stocks it will be mirroring the market.

An atypical point of view: Sheldon Jacobs believes that having 15 or more funds is acceptable. "There are an awful lot of ways to diversify and to reduce risk," he maintains. "Just look at index funds. Once, there was just one index fund, based on the Standard & Poor's 500. Now there are large-cap, medium-cap, and small-cap indexes. There are value and growth indexes. So there are a lot of ways to diversify, and if you have a large portfolio, your investments should be widely diversified."

Also on the high side was Stein, who thought 8 to 12 funds is fine: "Even within an area, like aggressive growth or income or high yield, I like to have a couple of different funds. I prefer to diversify more, and it doesn't cost extra to diversify. With high-yield funds, for example, I may buy shares of a fund with high-quality bonds and another with low-quality bonds."

Litman invests his clients in 8 to 12 funds, because he wants them to own a variety of funds with different investment styles. But unless the average investor wants to diversify among value, growth, and small-company funds, Littman might recommend only six to eight funds. The benefit of having funds wth different styles, Littman notes, is that over the long term they should all do well, even as particular styles go in and out of style.

Next question: Which types of funds should you *not* own? Specialty or sector funds were the most common choice: eight panelists would ignore sector funds. A few mentioned exceptions, though, like utility funds or health-care funds.

Says Jacobs, "I don't invest in anything I don't understand, and I don't understand sector funds. I mean, Merrill Lynch may have 30 industrial experts studying conditions full-time. Am I supposed to be an expert in 30 or 35 different sectors? We all know that you can't be guided by a sector's past performance. I prefer investing in a diversified mutual fund and letting the manager do the job of choosing the sectors. The portfolio manager of a diversified fund will have some discretion about what he invests in, but the manager of a sector fund can't do much if his sector hits the skids."

Besides, if you invest in a diversified fund with a three- or five-year record, Jacobs continues, you can have some confidence in the manager's abilities. Whereas if you invest in a sector fund with a good record, it may just mean that the manager was in the right place at the right time.

"Sector funds aren't for mutual fund investors," Jacobs concludes. "They're for stock investors."

CHAPTER 22 Assembling an Entire Portfolio

Stein also disdains "narrowly defined" sector funds, but not those that are broadly defined and that one might buy for the long term—technology funds, health-care funds, and real estate. "In general, though, I'm reluctant to invest in them," says Stein. "They'll have a hot hand for a while, then go cold. They change too fast."

Litman notes that the typical investor buys past performance, and with sector funds, the evidence is that buying the past is a recipe for disaster. "Let the manager of a diversified fund decide what sectors you should be in," he suggests.

Phillips was particularly scornful of government "plus" funds, which promised to provide the returns of junk bonds with the stability of Treasuries. (Most if not all have bitten the dust.) In general, he distinguishes between new funds launched by managers and those launched by marketers—and cites government plus funds as one hatched by marketers. What made them so appalling, he goes on, was that they attracted unsophisticated investors, just moving out of money market funds and certificates of deposit.

Aspersions were also cast on "new inventions, like ARM funds," and on option income funds. One panelist objected not just to sector funds but to asset allocation and to aggressive funds.

Paul Merriman, the market-timer, disdained volatile funds—unless they are timed.

Asked what types of funds they would use to construct a generic, diversified portfolio of funds, the panelists chose growth funds (16 for, no maybes, none against); small cap funds (13 yes, none no, and three maybes); growth and income funds (13 yes, none no, three maybes); international (13 yes, none no, 3 maybes); fixed income (13 yes, none no, 2 maybes); and equity income (9 yes, none no, 5 perhaps).

Beyond that, the panelists became a little skeptical. On balanced funds, the vote was 4 yes, 10 maybe, and 1 no. Aggressive growth funds had an even worse time: 7 yes, 8 maybe, and 1 no. On global: 5 yes, 1 no, 8 maybe. The most no votes were recorded by flexible funds: 4 yes, 6 no, 5 maybe.

Brouwer is dubious of equity-income funds because he believes that the category doesn't have clear-cut guidelines: That's why they differ markedly from one another. He's also dubious of growth-and-income funds and balanced funds: You probably can do better putting together superb growth funds and superb income funds yourself, he contends. Still, if an investor has only a small amount of money, Brouwer might suggest a balanced fund; and if the investor wants a conservative stock fund, Brouwer might suggest an equity-income fund.

Donoghue is doubtful about growth-and-income funds, equity-income funds, and balanced funds: "Basically," he says, "we want strong ingredients in our portfolios, not mush. You can create a balanced portfolio of volatile funds."

Although he is a rather opportunistic investor, Weber is skeptical of flexible funds, preferring that the investor himself do any switching. "There aren't many examples of successful market-timing funds," he said. "It's obviously more difficult to market-time a fund from the inside than from the outside. A portfolio manager might have to sell a hundred or two hundred stocks to shift to cash, and it will be very expensive for him; I can move to cash in one day with one phone call."

Higgins, a fairly opportunistic investor, also looks askance at flexible funds: "They do what I do," he explains. He wouldn't eliminate them entirely, but he believes that too much flexibility merges into a wishy-washy way of investing.

A patient investor, Skala is—naturally—not an admirer of flexible funds. (He calls them "asset allocation funds.") They thrived in 1987 after the crash, he notes, because they weren't heavily invested in the stock market, but "they were too cautious when the market took off again," some of them putting money into cash and real estate instead. "Besides," he adds, "such funds tend to have high expenses, what with so many different people studying different markets."

Weber is also skeptical of having small-company funds and equity-income funds in a portfolio, preferring to leave it to the managers of the growth funds he buys to decide whether to shift to small companies or to high-dividend payers.

Merriman doesn't have much truck with global or balanced funds. Investors should just pick their own domestic and international funds, he argues, and do their own asset allocations. He considers balanced funds "a chicken's way of investing, a way of hiding from reality." Still, he grudgingly grants that such neither-fish-nor-fowl funds may fulfill emotional needs: If stocks decline

CHAPTER 22 Assembling an Entire Portfolio

quickly, balanced funds won't go down so fast and so far, and thus may keep unsophisticated investors from panicking.

Aggressive-growth funds were on Berry's avoid list. "Unless you're a market-timer," he says, "you'll be blown away when they get hit—and when they get hit, they really get hit. When the stock market goes to hell, they go to hell with it." He recommends that investors stay with the better growth funds: "I'd invest in 20th Century Growth, but not 20th Century Ultra."

Berry is also dubious of asset-allocation funds, noting that they have not done well since the crash. The asset-allocation funds with fixed percentages in various areas won't do well unless all the areas do well: "Otherwise, they'll cancel each other out." As for flexible funds, "They have to go into the right sector at the right time, and there's no evidence that anyone is that smart."

Schabacker feels that long-term growth funds are where investors should concentrate. Aggressive-growth funds aren't worth buying: "Their risk outweighs their rewards." Global funds—those that buy domestic and foreign stocks—are also "not worth fooling with." You can create your own combination of good domestic and foreign funds.

As components of a portfolio, there were two write-in votes for junk-bond funds (presumably included in fixed income) and one write-in mention of gold funds: The panelist who suggested that gold funds be voted on later voted against them!

CHAPTER

Just Funds—or Individual Securities, Too?

Here are the comments from panelists who preferred portfolios exclusively composed of mutual funds:

- "Individual stocks and bonds are not needed."—Schabacker
- "The individual investor can achieve whatever objective he or she has with no-load mutual funds and will in most cases do far better given the same amount of time devoted to selecting and monitoring investments."—Litman
- "No, insufficient liquidity and diversification."—Donoghue
- "No, high trading costs (commissions, spreads); risk (lack of diversification); time required to research."—Brouwer
- "Only in extenuating circumstances, such as long-held stocks with accumulated gains, or if an investor actively enjoys the game of stock-picking."—Stein
- "Exception: stocks that he knows more about than Wall Street."—Jacobs

Here were comments from panelists who approved of investors owning individual securities:

- "Any investor who develops an interest in stocks or bonds through funds should feel free to buy individual securities to round out a portfolio."—Phillips
- "Yes, if he has firsthand knowledge of a company or industry."—Higgins
- "Direct ownership develops experience in selecting and monitoring investments; [it's a] way to participate more directly in companies with [a] promising future."—Skala

Then there were panelists who approved mainly of investors owning individual bonds:

- "I pick up a top-yielding bond for income once or twice a year."—Pope
- "Stocks, no. Most do better with funds. Bonds, yes, if there's enough money to buy a portfolio—because of guaranteed maturity price. Smaller bond investors need diversification only available through funds."—Berry
- "Depends on temperament of investor. Individual bonds (U.S.) generally OK. Stock funds probably better than individual stocks."—Droms

The explanations suggested that the views were not so polarized as they seemed at first. A panelist voting yes ("If he has firsthand knowledge of a company or industry") could have voted no, agreeing with the panelist who provided as an exception "stocks that he knows more about than Wall Street."

The overall verdict: a strong bias toward stock funds, a slight bias toward fixed-income funds.

CHAPTER 24

A Typology of Market-Timers

Most investors, if you get them into a dark room and torture them long enough, will confess that they market-time. After all, one can make a good case that even dollar-cost averaging is a version of market-timing, milk-and-watery though it may be. (Broadly speaking, market-timing means trying to avoid bear markets and trying to participate in bull markets.)

Market-timing has a bad name, and probably for good reason. It's not something that beginning investors should practice. For amateurs, market-timing tends to mean buying high and selling low. They buy when almost everyone is euphoric; they sell when all they hear are the nattering nabobs of negativism.

Probably the most sophisticated market-timers are investors who recognize how difficult it is to predict the market's future behavior accurately, and seldom, if ever, make really big bets about the market's direction.

The antithesis of a market-timer is a buy-and-holder—someone who is fully invested all the time and who probably believes in the efficient-market theory: the notion that stocks are always, or almost always, reasonably priced. If stocks are always reasonably priced, or almost always reasonably priced, why market-time? Days like October 19, 1987, when the Dow Jones Industrial Average abruptly shed 508 points, just cannot happen.

Then there's the question of whether you're market-timing when you buy shares of stocks near or at their yearly low and sell them near or at their yearly high. That's what value investing is all about. The argument can be made that it's a cousin of market-timing—you're practicing timing, but you're not timing the entire market. Still, it's not a big leap from looking for points at which a stock is cheap or expensive and looking for points at which a group of stocks are cheap or expensive.

But let's concede, for argument's sake, that dollar-cost averaging isn't a passive form of market-timing (comparable to moving in and out of the market according to 200-day moving averages), and concede, too, that timing individual stocks isn't quite the same as market-timing, either.

The truth remains that more people market-time than will admit it. Market-timing has a nasty name; in the world of investing, it represents what astrology represents to the world of astronomy.

Interviewing one investor not long ago, I asked whether he market-timed at all. He chuckled. Silly question. Of course not. Later I asked him how he was positioned—and he answered that he was 43% in cash because he thought the stock market was vastly overvalued.

Another time, I interviewed Tom Bailey, who launched the Janus Fund in 1970 and guided it so capably over the years. I told him how much I admired him for being such a skillful market-timer that he had avoided the bloodbath of 1972–73, when the stock market lost 48% of its value. He hit the ceiling: Only journalists like me called him a market-timer, he informed me angrily. He wasn't a market-timer. It's just that when he didn't see any good buys available, he didn't buy anything.

The problem is that there are degrees of market-timing—from weak and watery to aggressive and audacious. You're a restrained market-timer if you let more cash than usual accumulate in your portfolio at certain times or buy blue-chip stocks rather than small companies at other times. You're an aggressive market-timer if you buy puts and calls on market indexes at certain times, or sell short or buy on margin at other times.

CHAPTER 24 A Typology of Market-Timers

Degrees of market-timing also vary according to the signals you pay attention to. If you're guided by such overt signals as the fact that you just can't find bargains (or bargains abound), or the average price-earnings ratio of the S&P 500 is at an all-time high (or low), you're a restrained market-timer. You're an aggressive market-timer if you think the economy is slipping (or climbing) and stocks will follow: That's the boldest kind of prediction.

Below is a typology of market-timers, divided according to the steps they take when they think stocks are too high or too low—and how they determine whether stocks are too high or too low.

A restrained market-timer would be a 1-A. An aggressive market-timer would be a 6-F. (You can, of course, market-time in the bond market, with commodities, and so forth. And you could be any combination—1-F, 3-A, and so forth.)

If one invests in mutual funds that market-time, then the fund managers are your agents—and what degree of market-timer you are depends on the strategies and tactics of the funds you invest in.

Market-Timing Signals

Restrained   *Aggressive*
1. No good bargains/a lot of bargains (bottom up)
   2. Market indicators (like p-e ratios and dividend yields) suggest that prices are high/low
      3. Signs that sentiment is turning negative or positive
         4. Stock prices are slipping or climbing
            5. Economy is slipping or prospering
               6. Economy is about to slip or quicken (top down)

Steps

Restrained   *Aggressive*
A. Move slightly into more conservative/more aggressive stocks
   B. Hold (or invest) a little more cash
      C. Go heavily into more conservative-more aggressive stocks or funds
         D. Sell/buy a lot more stocks
            E. Buy puts/calls
               F. Sell short/buy on margin

Whether or not market-timing works is something else again. The evidence of Mark Hulbert, who publishes a newsletter that evaluates newsletters' performances, is that it seems to work for certain investors, particularly those who limit the number of their major moves. That seems logical. Going in and out of the market all the time doesn't seem as provident as just making major moves at what are clearly extreme points—as in October of 1987.

Of course, while certain investors are unarguably successful market-timers—Martin Zweig, for instance—the official response is that the number of successful market-timers equals the number that you would expect purely by chance. (Just as the percentage of top-performing funds is the number predicted by chance.)

The academic arguments against market-timing consist of:

- Market-timing costs a fortune in commissions. (Answer: Not if you buy no-load mutual funds.)
- If you miss a few key rallies, you won't have benefited from a bull market. (Answer: The market can go down rather swiftly, too. And who said that your entire portfolio must be market-timed?)

Then there's the question of how to prove whether market-timing works. If you say to a timer, "Your total return was less over five years than the S&P 500," his or her slippery response may be: "Yes, but I was out of the market some of that time, so I protected you from the risk of a major downturn."

Whether or not market-timing works seems to depend on whether the timer adds value—whether his or her total return, in view of the volatility of the portfolio, produced an impressive risk-adjusted return.

The mutual-fund panelists were asked to identify their own positions along the market-timing continuum, from absolute buy-and-holders to strong market-timers. As phrased, the question was: "Stock-market-timers may be absolute (e.g., retreating entirely to cash in expectation of a bear market); strong (selling almost all stocks if a decline seems to have started); or mild (lightening up in expectation of a bear market, or in case they can't find well-priced, good stocks, or moving to more conservative stocks, or letting cash build up if they cannot find good buys). Or they

CHAPTER 24 A Typology of Market-Timers

may not be market-timers at all (they may always be fully invested in the stocks they normally buy)."

Asked to rate themselves from 1 (absolute) to 7 (always fully invested), here is how the panelists voted:

One gave himself a 1 (absolute); one gave himself a 2 (between strong and absolute); one gave himself a 3 (strong); three gave themselves a 4 (between mild and strong); six gave themselves a 5 (mild); two gave themselves a 6 (between mild and always fully invested); one gave himself a 6.5; and two gave themselves a 7 (always fully invested).

The two panelists who had rated themselves as 7s (Ram Kolluri and Don Phillips) were buy-and-holders. Kolluri rated himself slightly below patient, Phillips was fully patient. The panelist who gave himself a 6.5, Litman, also considered himself patient; the panelist who gave himself a 6, Droms, also considered himself patient. Berry, who also gave himself a 6, was the chief exception: He listed himself as a notch below opportunistic.

Berry's strategy is to move from top-performing fund to top-performing fund. He is certainly not a buy-and-holder—yet he vehemently denies being a market-timer. "Market-timers are just a notch above buy-and-holders," he says contemptuously. "And buy-and-holders are at the bottom."

While Berry doesn't fit neatly into the typology sketched above, he might be a 3—except that he's dubious of aggressive mutual funds. And he might be a C—in the sense that he's guided by what investors are actually buying or selling.

The absolute market-timer, Merriman, was also absolutely opportunistic. But one panelist (Donoghue) who indicated that he was a strong market-timer also considered himself an all-but-patient investor.

The market-timers/opportunists were also likely to sell poor-performing funds quickly, while the buy-and-holders were likely to give poor-performing funds more leeway.

Curiously, several of the market-timers, along with a few buy-and-holders, were reluctant to buy market-timing funds—"flexible" or "aggressive asset-allocation funds." Asked to construct a generic portfolio of various types of funds, more panelists (six) indicated that they were more likely not to include a flexible fund than any other type of fund, and the majority of the six were the opportunistic, market-timing panelists. (Five said that they *might* include such a fund, and four that they would.)

The market-timers opposed to flexible funds had a ready explanation: *They* want to do the timing. The portfolio managers, these panelists feel, had other things they should be doing.

SECTION IV

INTERVIEWS WITH 17 TOP MANAGERS

The mutual fund experts interviewed for this book are like managers of baseball teams. While they themselves don't actually run any mutual funds, they're pretty good at choosing the better players and assembling entire teams.

Now it's time to talk to some of the players themselves. They will describe their own investment strategies, of course, but also deal with some of the questions that the fund experts grappled with: How many funds should you own? When should you sell a fund? Why do some managers excel while others fall on their faces?

Baseball managers often choose different All-Star players from the ones the players themselves choose. But the views of the majority of the mutual fund experts and the mutual fund managers turned out to be, so to speak, in the same ballpark.

CHAPTER 25

Vanguard's John Bogle: "No Ifs, Ands, or Buts. Buy an Index Fund."

If I tell you that I occasionally get lost in the morning wending my way from my bedroom to the kitchen, you will have a faint idea of how poor my sense of direction is and will therefore sympathize with me for being an hour late for my appointment with John C. Bogle in Valley Forge, Pennsylvania.

Would he be furious? Would he have left his office in a huff?

But the chairman and founder of the Vanguard Group of mutual funds was there, friendly, charming, and—every writer's dream—recalling some things I had written about him and chuckling in appreciation.

Bogle is one of my heroes, a man who—in an age when Machiavellianism seems to have run amok and everybody's [a Saddam Hussein]—has integrity and isn't ashamed of it.

The name "Vanguard" has become synonymous with rectitude. It's a mutual fund family, owned by its shareholders, that practices a version of thrift not seen since the days of Ebenezer Scrooge, and whose lofty moral standards have prompted it to caution its own investors—at appropriate times—against junk bonds, against health-care funds, and against Standard & Poor's index funds.

The idyllic Vanguard headquarters, built in 1993, consists of several low and long brick buildings, all named after English ships that flourished during the Napoleonic Wars. (Vanguard was such a ship.) Bogle, after all, had run Wellington Management before starting Vanguard—and was fired from Vanguard for being, apparently, too demanding. (Wellington nonetheless manages many Vanguard funds.)

People call the place the "campus," and it sure looks like one. There's a big cafeteria where everyone, including John Bogle, eats. The friendly chap who escorted me around pointed out, among other things, a walkway called (prepare to groan) the Random Walk.

Bogle loves funds that model themselves on the Standard & Poor's 500 Stock Index or other indexes, and Vanguard offers a variety of them. He urges beginning investors to try an index fund on for size. "No ifs, ands, or buts. Buy an index fund, watch it go up and down, and don't worry about manager reports—'We bought X and we sold Y.' It's not valuable information." An S&P index fund with low expenses, he notes, will outperform 75% of all other stock mutual funds.

He also loves funds that have low expenses, something Vanguard is famous for. The difference in the performance of money market funds, he argues, is accounted for entirely by their expenses. With fixed-income funds, he reports, expenses account for 75% to 80% of any differences in performance; with stock funds, probably 60% of any difference.

Something that worries him about mutual funds is the pace at which people buy and sell shares. The redemption rate among no-load funds is 25% to 27% a year, he pointed out, although it's only 11% at Vanguard funds.

"Back in my old days," he said, "the redemption rate was 6 to 8%, which meant that the average investor held on for 15 or so years. Now the average investor holds on for 2.7 years. There's too much exchanging, too much redeeming, too much jumping on the bandwagon. Investors aren't letting mutual funds do what they're supposed to do—to make money for them."

I asked about the new, more adventurous funds that Vanguard has launched, called the Horizon funds.

"Up to now, we haven't offered investors an alternative to essentially a very conservative investment program," Bogle replied.

CHAPTER 25 Vanguard's John Bogle

"And we continue to believe that a core portfolio should consist of a stock index fund, a bond index fund, along with maybe our Windsor Fund, our U.S. Growth Fund, and long-term Treasury bonds.

"But we thought we should make available a few more funds. One of our largest competitors has 46 aggressive-growth funds, and we have four. Well, we're going all the way to eight. So we won't be in that league. That's a good league if you want hyped short-term performance."

"That other family is Fidelity?" I asked innocently.

"I never talk about Fidelity—and name them," he said with a laugh. "But you're on the right track."

Vanguard's aggressive stock funds will, naturally, have unusually low expenses.

"While our new funds will be a little more aggressive," Bogle went on, "they won't be heavily promoted, partly because we think that Vanguard has built a niche in the low-cost area that needs to be filled, and if people don't want to buy our new funds, we'll respect that. We're far more conservative than Fidelity, and I don't say that in a pejorative way.

"But they're now following our bond strategy, which is: Don't play games with bonds. But it will be a long time before they follow our stock strategy. They want to be much more aggressive. Fine, we have no objection to that. These are all business decisions.

"In the long run," he continued, "what kills you in the mutual fund business, the Achilles' heel, is volatility. When a fund goes from $10 to $30, everyone starts buying it. And then it goes down to $20, but it still shows a 100% gain. Yet the average investor in that fund, who bought at $30, has lost one-third of his money. And heavily publicizing that volatile fund isn't good marketing strategy.

"Fidelity knows and cares more about modern marketing than I will ever know," he went on. "I just plain don't like marketing. I think that doing what's right—and I know that this sounds funny—I think that doing what's right will bring you out in the end where you want to go."

CHAPTER 26

PBHG's Gary Pilgrim: "You Get Too Attached to These Companies."

A Chartered Financial Analyst, Gary L. Pilgrim received a B.S. degree from the University of Tulsa and an M.B.A. from Drexel. He became the chief investment officer of Pilgrim Baxter & Associates in 1982. PBHG has recently started a variety of different funds.

Q. Are PBHG Growth and Emerging Growth identical?

A. I think it's fair to say they are identical. The portfolio characteristics, the philosophy, the stock-picking strategy techniques, number of securities, etc., . . . all very similar indeed, except for the size of the companies.

When the small funds' companies reach about $700 million in market cap, they're sold. My fund, the PBHG Growth Fund, when they reach $2 billion, they're sold. And of course there's lots of room for managing positions up to that limit, but the average composite market cap of the PBHG Growth Fund runs around $650 or so and runs around $250 to $300 in the smaller-company fund. So it really is just a focus on different-sized companies at different stages of their growth.

Q. Are there any subtle differences in managing these two funds? It seems to me that with Emerging Growth you know that the stocks are smaller and less liquid, and you can move the market too much, I guess, by buying too much too soon.

A. In both cases, these funds invest in the smaller part of the market. It is a less liquid part of the market. The holdings of companies like this tend to be more concentrated because they have fewer shareholders and there are fewer market-makers in the over-the-counter markets for these securities.

The subtle differences would be hard for me to pinpoint because the approach to managing them is identical. Maybe the subtle difference is that Chris Baxter [who runs Emerging Growth] is a better manager than I am.

Q. Chris once told me that she sells some stocks and then in many cases buys them back. Apparently she sells them because she was worried about them and then her worries were resolved.

A. Oh, we all do that. Our approach to these kinds of companies recognizes that they are higher risk than more mature companies and that it's very difficult to have a lot of confidence as to how far and how high and how long they're going to have exceptional growth. So, if we suspect there's a major uncertainty that we can't resolve, we are quick to sell. We will stand on the sidelines until we're more comfortable that things are OK.

It's better to shoot first and ask questions later with a lot of these kinds of companies, where you literally can't have a high level of confidence. And, of course, you never get the bad news until it's too late with some of these companies, and the volatility is outrageously sharp when you get bad news. We try to manage that uncertainty with that kind of risk-averse attitude.

Q. It seems to me that what differentiates growth managers who do very well and those that don't do very well is, to a large extent, the fact that the better managers are very quick to cut the cord. You have to sell just before everyone else thinks of selling.

A. Well, you know, that's the ideal outcome, to be able to anticipate negative developments and be very sensitive to that. The other thing that's always tempting to do, which I think hurts all of us growth managers, is you get too attached to these companies, and you get some bad news, and the company convinces you that everything will be just fine if you'll be patient. And the next thing you know, your stock's off 30 or 40%; then they have the bad quarter, then another couple of months go by and you keep waiting for things to get better. And you wind up selling the stock down 60 or 70%; and you've wasted six or nine months of opportunity cost. You have to be constantly vigilant to that trap. And it's very difficult to wake up every day and say, "Hey, it's a new day; I'm going to deal with these facts as I see them today. And if this company is faltering, then it deserves to be out of the portfolio and replaced with something that looks a little more sure."

Q. Gary, how many stocks can a person watch over? What's the absolute limit? How many stocks do you have in your portfolios?

A. I have currently about 90 stocks in the PBHG Growth Fund, and I think Chrissy has probably 85 or so. It's pretty similar.

Q. Do you think that's the maximum? Someone once told me that 100 is the maximum.

A. I don't think there is any limit to how many stocks an organization can keep track of if it's properly staffed and organized to process information. But I think an individual who does investing part-time while he's busy trying to make a living faces an entirely different dilemma. And I don't think you can keep up with one stock in that sense if you're primarily doing something else. Because during the course of every day, there's a tremendous amount of information being communicated to institutional shareholders from the company, from analysts, from all different directions. To stay very well informed about your portfolio is more than a full-time job.

Q. You follow a quantitative approach, or mainly a quantitative approach, looking at the fundamentals, at the numbers. That's true, isn't it?

A. I would have characterized it slightly differently. We don't think of ourselves as quantitative managers in a black-box system sort of way. We think of ourselves as having developed some very good productivity tools to process information that allows us to then turn around and rank the stocks that we follow.

We follow around 800 companies, but to rank them in a way that constantly draws our attention to which of these very good companies are doing the best in terms of current earnings surprises, current earnings growth, current earnings estimate, revisions, and so forth; so we've been able to create models that allow us to monitor a tremendous amount of information and compare our companies against one another to be sure we're always investing in the best of a good bunch.

Q. So it's mainly by the numbers, but you also look at what's going on in the field.

A. Oh, yes. The number crunching, for lack of a better phrase, the organization of all this information—it allows us to have a good starting point, to apply the art form of individual company assessment to the process. If I have 800 stocks to look at and I want to buy only from the top 20 or 30% and I want to concentrate a portfolio in 80 or 90 stocks, I have to figure out—based on my judgment, experience, and understanding of what makes a company tick—to finally get it down to the number of stocks that I really want to own. The systems we employ just help us process and organize information so we can spend our analytical time on the highest-probability companies.

Q. What are your chief screens? What do you look for mainly in a small company?

A. To put a company into our internal universe of companies— and that's the 800 stocks that I referred to; that's Pilgrim Baxter's list of 800 of the best companies we can find in the domestic economy— we tend to look for very high returns on equity; good, solid balance sheets; a lot of internal financing capability; the reinvestment rate that a company has; the profit margins; and the actual growth. We like to see companies that have grown at least 20%. Most of our companies are growing much more rapidly than that. And we like to have some confidence that we're dealing with management that's shareholder-oriented, that has some sort of advantage in the areas that they operate in, so that their growth looks sustainable. Those are kind of the overall quality, growth/profitability characteristics that we look for.

Then we put these companies through our ranking system that looks at these other attributes of earnings acceleration, estimate revision, earnings surprises, and so forth, to try to figure out which of these companies are doing the best currently.

Q. I see. I heard recently that if a manager looks at only companies that are growing, say, at 50% a year, it might sound wonderful but it's rather dangerous to invest in a lot of companies that are growing at 50% a year because they can have a great big fall.

A. Well, I think the problem with very high growth-rate companies is that at some point they're going to slow down. And we don't pretend that we know how long an exceptional growth rate can be sustained—which is why we use all these techniques to monitor very short-term corporate performance, because if you say you don't know the future, then you better pay a lot of attention to the present and make sure that things are on track.

A 50% growth company is very common and typical in the world of companies that we're following. But a lot of those companies will have faltered three, four, five years from now, and we're trying to own them during those periods when they've had that exceptional growth, and people are raising their expectations for the company's longer-term outlook. And then as they do that, the stocks usually expand their p/e's, and expand their earnings, and so forth, and that's how you make your three and four times on your money.

But you're going to have accidents in this part of the world. And if we get it right 60% of the time, we'll make a lot of money. You have to be prepared that probably every now and then—at least two or three times a quarter—you're going to have a company that gives you a negative surprise, and the stocks are going to go down 30% on the day of the news. That's the part of the world that we're operating in.

And we're stoic about that. Companies always hope that they're going to do well, and they're slow to admit when things aren't working out. They're very optimistic sorts of companies.

CHAPTER 27

Loomis-Sayles' Dan Fuss: "I Don't Even Have a Computer in My Office."

Daniel J. Fuss buys anything that's cheap, from "busted" convertibles to New Zealand bonds. But while he's not (so to speak) extremely fussy about what he buys, his returns have been spectacular.

Q. What is your investment style?
A. Miscellaneous. We're completely flexible. We invest in a lot of things that people might find strange. That's because we'll go wherever we find cheap bonds.

We've done a lot of "correlations," trying to find out what type of investment our fund most resembles: High-yield bonds? Foreign bonds? Nothing matches. Our marketing people would love it if we fell into a category. They could go out and say, "Hey, the Loomis Bond Fund buys this and that." Most people looking to hire money managers aren't looking for "miscellaneous" managers. But that's our style: looking for cheap bonds up and down the yield curve.

Our real worry is reinvestment risk. We don't want to have to invest money when interest rates are down. We want to maintain our level of income, hoping that our securities climb in value at the same time.

Reinvestment risk is what we consider "going-out-of-business" risk. I refuse to let that risk climb.

So our holdings tend to have long maturities. And we have an aversion to bonds that can be called—bonds that the issuer can pay off early when interest rates go down.

What we really love are deep-discount bonds. They're not going to be paid off early. Actually, if they were called, we'd throw a party. If you bought a discount bond at $80 a unit, the issuer would have to pay it off at $100.

Another good thing is that if you choose deep-discount bonds wisely, the credit quality of the companies issuing them should improve. What we like to do is buy a bond at $80, and—as the credit quality is upgraded—watch as its value rises to $85, $86, or $87.

Q. Are there any fixed-income investments you're biased against?

A. We're dubious of mortgages. You never know when you're going to get your money back, when homeowners will decide to pay off their mortgages because interest rates have gone down. But occasionally we'll pick up deep-discount mortgages, which are unlikely to be paid off early.

Q. What's your turnover?

A. For a fund that's flexible, we don't move around a lot. Our holdings remain pretty much the same. Our turnover is only 87%, very low for a bond fund. The average turnover last year for a fixed-income fund was about 162 percent.

Q. What about your funds' volatility?

A. Our volatility isn't especially high, either, even though we tend to buy for the long term. In normal markets, we don't seem to bounce around much. Our volatility is like that of an intermediate-long-term bond, not the greater volatility of a long-term bond.

The reason is that much of what we buy doesn't track the bond market itself—such as adjustable-rate preferred stocks and deep-discount bonds. We have a lot of strange things, and they don't tend to bounce up and down like conventional bonds.

Q. What about your fund's credit quality?

A. It's about average: BAA. It tends to creep up if we don't see much advantage being in corporates rather than safer Treasuries. The last time that happened was late 1993–early 1994, when I just couldn't find deep discounts in corporate bonds.

CHAPTER 27 Loomis-Sayles' Dan Fuss

We're allowed to have 35% of the fund in high-yielding bonds. If you're diversified, the principal risk is liquidity. In 1990, you'll remember, there was a panic and almost everyone sold their junk bonds. So you had to be able to hold on and not be forced to raise to cash. We did that—and survived quite well.

To invest in low-rated bonds successfully, you need good research—and that's what we're strong on. We have a large research department. Busted convertibles make up a lot of our low-rated holdings, and that's an area where our good research can pick up sleepers. Not a lot of bond analysts follow busted converts. (Busted convertibles: Those that are selling at low prices because the stock's price is also so far down that converting the bond to the stock isn't worth it.)

Q. When do you sell?

A. We sell our holdings when they're no longer cheap. It's that simple. Normally the process takes two or two and a half years. It can take five years; once in a while, it takes only six months. What happens is either that other investors discover the bonds; or, at the time that we discover the bonds and buy them, other investors hesitate.

Q. Do you try to predict interest rates?

A. We don't market-time, or try to predict the direction of interest rates. But you always have a forecast up your sleeve. People who pay you money don't expect you to tell them, "I don't know where interest rates are going." But in reality, if you're buying bonds across the yield curve, you need an implicit forecast. If we see the wind blowing very strongly, and it's abundantly clear that interest rates are going one way or another, we'll lean one way or another. But the bond market doesn't correct instantaneously. There can be a long lag. So you don't have to make abrupt, jarring, expensive changes.

Q. How good are you at predicting interest rates?

A. Lousy. My mistake is that I tend to be very early. But I don't go betting a lot of money on my forecasts. What I'm darned good at is seeing where things are now, where the best bargains are.

Q. Is your fund as big as you want it to be?

A. For us, size isn't a concern. We're not looking to get the first crack at new issues, so we don't have to be considered the biggest player on the block. Our only worry is that the fund might get too big too quickly. We like slow, steady growth, so we couldn't invest all that money properly.

Q. Would you say that your fund is aggressive?

A. Our fund, frankly, does take some risks, but we're so broadly diversified that we're not vulnerable to any single risk. My own money is mostly in the fund. My secretary has all of her money in it, and so does my father-in-law. So you can see why I want to keep an eye on the riskiness.

We work especially hard on this fund because its our flagship fund. Loomis-Sayles doesn't do any advertising. It relies on word of mouth. So the bond fund in effect is our advertising campaign.

I don't think you have to be a math whiz to succeed in the bond business. I'm reasonably quick with numbers, but I don't even have a computer in my office. I use a slide rule. Bonds are not that mathematically precise. There's nothing precise about future cash flows.

My personal hero is Phil Carret, the 98-year-old money manager who started the Pioneer funds. He has all the qualities that you need to be an outstanding fixed-income manager. It's called experience.

CHAPTER 28

T. Rowe Price's Brian Rogers: "We're Willing to Take the Heat."

Brian C. Rogers has been running T. Rowe Price Equity-Income since 1985. He's a Chartered Financial Analyst with a B.A. and an M.B.A. from Harvard.

Q. In response to my questionnaire, your fund got the most votes—nine—of any fund, and it was voted the best equity-income fund.

A. That's good, I guess.

Q. The obvious question is, why has your fund done so much better than other equity-income funds?

A. I think it's a combination of basically just being sufficiently contrarian over the years and relatively consistent in terms of our approach. If I went back and looked at 10 of our annual reports, we do the same kind of thing all the time. We buy things that have been a little bit troubled in the marketplace, and consequently, their yields are up. A lot of our analysis tries to get to the issue of, "Will something change? Will investor perception improve? Will the stock price respond accordingly over a couple of years?"

We haven't really done anything extreme. We've tended to be pretty conservative, both in terms of diversification and in the types of companies we invest in—really large-caps. We have the courage of our convictions to go into something really controversial, and we're willing to take the heat, short-term, in pursuit of good long-term returns.

We got a lot of heat for investing in the drug stocks in 1993, because of the spectre of health care reform. But they are probably the best investments we made in the last three years at this point. Now we've begun to cut back on some of those positions because they've done so well and their yields are down. We're looking for the next controversy.

So I think it's just a question of being consistent, being contrarian, and having a sufficient value bias.

Q. Some other equity-income funds have low yields, apparently because they're buying growth stocks....

A. In the equity-income universe, there are funds that have more in the way of growth stocks and lower yields than ours. At the other extreme are funds that have higher exposure on average to electric utilities than we would have, and consequently, higher yields than we have. We don't necessarily want to have holdings in any one sector, like electric utilities, all the time. Even a hypothesized growth stock, Eli Lilly, was once undervalued and yielding 5%—in 1993.

We're not real dogmatic in the fund, saying that we should always have 20% in electrical utilities because all yield 6 or 7%. There are times when utility yields look attractive to us and times when they don't.

Q. So your fund is consistent . . . and flexible.

A. We also look at how a company's dividend yield pattern has varied relative to its history. If Eli Lilly had a 5% yield in 1993—a higher yield relative to the market than Eli Lilly ever had—we'd be interested. Conversely, something like Baltimore Gas and Electric, even though it yields 6.5%, may be real attractive at times and other times that yield may not be attractive in historical terms. So we try to focus on how dividend patterns vary to determine when yields are cheap and when they are a little low.

Q. A stock can have a very high yield and be properly valued, can't it? It can be very risky.

A. Oh yeah. Some not-successful investments have been among the absolutely highest-yielding stocks when we bought them. They got into trouble or the dividend got into trouble. So we try to avoid the temptation of stretching for yield because, from time to time, stretching for yield can get you into trouble. Some companies have very high yields and deservedly so.

Higher yield doesn't have to mean undervalued, but in general, higher-than-average yields are an attribute of undervalued securities.

We diversify pretty broadly. It's tough for us to know exactly where our performance is going to come from, whether it's holding number 1 or holding number 20. And when you pursue a value strategy, you have to make a number of bets because you don't know when investors are going to view a company more favorably.

Q. Your fund has a very low turnover. When do you sell?

A. We've always told folks, we have a three-year horizon. Sometimes it takes time for the perception of a company to change. We'll collect a 3 to 4 to 5% yield in this low-yielding environment from a stock with the potential to do real well—over the next month or next 30 months. You have to be patient.

Q. When do you throw in the towel?

A. What worries me most is if the financials and balance-sheet strength deteriorate, if there's a never-ending turnaround. I'll be candid in saying that some things don't turn, or take forever to turn. We also consider selling if one of our 25 odd analysts—no, I shouldn't call them odd—if one of our 25 or so analysts has a negative opinion ... because of a lousy merger, a management change, anything. A third reason is if we decide there's real serious earnings or dividend risk.

We may sell a stock even if it's done well—"portfolio recycling." A stock's absolute and relative yield patterns may be less attractive when the price has gone up.

Q. Is it different now, investing in a low-dividend environment?

A. It makes stock selection a little tougher. We're a bit more sensitive to not taking too much risk. A low yield may mean not much market-return potential.

Q. What about the danger that a troubled company with a high dividend may cut its dividend?

A. Hopefully, we won't be in too many of those situations. But inevitably you hit the wall from time to time. But times when companies have cut their dividends, in my experience, the stock is at or near its inflection point. You've paid the piper. So we don't automatically sell if a company cuts its dividend. Others may be doing that. Believe it or not, we've had decent experiences after dividend cuts. They're often accompanied by some management change, a restructuring, sale of a division, or a stock buyback.

Usually a cut in dividends is a sign of maximum stress, and it usually means that a stock has done as badly—in a relative sense—as it's going to. So we're inclined to wait before extracting ourself. Oftentimes it's just water under the bridge.

CHAPTER 29

T. Rowe Price's Preston Athey: "It's Not a Glamorous Way to Invest."

Preston Athey, manager of T. Rowe Price Small Cap Value Fund, received a bachelor's degree from Yale in 1971 and an M.B.A. from Stanford in 1978. The fund closed to new investors March 1, 1996—without warning. This interview was conducted before the fund closed.

Q. Why did you decide to reopen the fund in 1995?
A. The main reason really goes back to why we closed the fund in 1993. At that time, the small cap stocks had had a very good run in the stock market. There were a lot of investors who were interested in the area, and frankly, we had done a pretty good job and were blessed with an overabundance of cash flow from new investors. And that cash flow came in at such a rate that we found it difficult, if not impossible, to invest it in the patient way that is the hallmark of the kind of investing that we do in the Small Cap Value Fund.

So rather than change our style or allow the cash to build up to an unreasonably high level, we decided to close the fund to new investors and protect current shareholders. Over the subsequent two years, we were able to invest the cash that had come in. And in the meantime, the small company stocks sector began to cool off. We found a lot of bargains, very interesting companies that we wanted to buy. And therefore [in 1995], we thought that we could reopen it, handle any additional cash that might come in, and do so in the prudent way that makes sense in the value investing style.

Q. Would you close the fund again if money started pouring in too quickly?

A. Well, we have not obviously set a closing date and we have not set any level at which we would close it, but I guess the best way to answer is we did it once and it's probable that we would do it again if the same circumstances arose.

Q. I suppose that one of the problems with running a small company fund is that if you have too much money coming in, you can try to buy a great many small company stocks, but at some point it becomes very difficult to manage a portfolio of hundreds and hundreds of small company stocks.

A. Well, I think that's true. Of course, if you're able to do it carefully and you have a good analytical group, such as we have at T. Rowe Price, it's easier than if I had to do all the work myself, following every single company in the fund.

It is true that if you want to be an active manager and have a good knowledge of each company, there's only so many you can do that with before your span of control gets a little away from you.

Q. I recently heard someone estimate how many stocks a portfolio manager can keep track of. I think it was about 100. What would you say?

A. I think you know the number could be anywhere from 10 or 15 right on up to well more than 100. I'm sure that Peter Lynch was well on top of most of the companies in Magellan Fund, and when he left, I think there were well over 2,000 stocks in the portfolio. But Peter also worked very, very hard and spent a lot of hours every week reading annual reports and staying on top of his companies.

I think it's, frankly, just a function of how hard you want to work.

Q. I asked Peter Lynch once if he could name every stock he had in his fund. And this was a time he was buying bank stocks. And he said, "I have 100 bank stocks that begin with the word 'First.' " He couldn't come anywhere near naming them all.

CHAPTER 29 T. Rowe Price's Preston Athey

Technology stocks have been beating the band. Why isn't your fund much heavier in technology than it is right now?

A. I am not biased against technology in any particular way. What I try to do, though, is look for value in the stock market. In my experience, value tends to occur when there's either a misunderstanding of a company or an industry, or that industry is out of favor for various reasons having to do with the fundamentals of sales and earnings growth.

Technology, as you rightly point out, has been doing very well. It's quite heavily owned by most managers and it's been probably the best-performing sector over the last two years of any in the whole stock market. When you take that as a background, I find it difficult to find what I call good values in that sector of the market. But I can certainly remember in past years when technology was out of favor; people who had invested in it sold their stocks and gave up. I can even remember one person say, "I'll never invest in another technology stock as long as I live." Well, of course, that's music to a value investor's ears, and if we ever have that day come again, I'd probably have a much higher weighting in technology.

Q. You do have an excellent record, despite your not having that many technology stocks. What do you do differently, and how is your fund different from other funds that invest in small companies?

A. The typical small-company fund in the United States today is a growth-oriented fund. I would guess that two-thirds of all the mutual funds that specialize in small companies invest in growth stocks. It's not because two-thirds of the companies available to them are growth companies. I think it just has to do with the public's attraction to companies that are going to be the next Microsoft or Apple or Wal-Mart or something of that type. And, clearly, if you can buy those companies early and avoid the inevitable torpedoes, as we call them—the companies that don't grow up, but instead blow up—then you can have a very good record over time.

What my fund tries to do, however, is to search out those companies—and there are many thousands of them, frankly—that are underappreciated, not followed well by Wall Street analysts, and sell at low price earnings or price-to-book ratios. Typically, the companies we invest in are not high-growth companies. They're generally not even household names. And as a result, we find that there are good values there, and if you're willing to be a patient buy-and-hold investor, over time you can make some very good money.

I have to tell you, it's not a glamorous way to invest. In fact, some have even called it a boring way to invest. At the end of the day, the tortoise often wins the race against the hare. And I guess we follow a tortoise style of investing.

Q. Your fund has a very low turnover. You don't buy and sell that often. I think your turnover was about 21% last year.

A. That's correct.

Q. That's probably very unusual for a small company fund, but probably to be expected from a small company fund that looks for undervalued stocks.

A. Clearly, the value investment community, I think, tends to have a lower turnover than the growth style. But our fund has an even lower turnover than even most of our competitors. And again I think that's because with good analytical work on the front end, we know the companies we invest in, we buy them at a good price, and we can afford to be patient, allowing for the natural forces within the companies and their industries to work to our advantage.

Q. Something else that distinguishes your fund is that you're pretty well diversified. You don't make big sector bets.

A. That's correct.

Q. It's a rather conservative small company fund then.

A. It's a very conservative small company fund. And frankly, we run it that way. I guess I can explain that by using an analogy.

As you know, one of the most interesting areas in the stock market to invest is small companies. But we also know from past experience that they tend to be quite volatile. I think that the average investor will often make a good decision to go into an area such as small companies, but may be taken by surprise by how volatile the stocks can be both on the upside and the downside. The worst thing that can happen to an investor is to buy high and sell low. And my experience has been that the greater the differential between the high price and the low price, the more anxious that the average investor will become, and there is always that danger that he or she will come to the day when they say, "Gee, my investment is down 30%; I wonder if it's going to zero." They panic and sell at the bottom.

CHAPTER 29 T. Rowe Price's Preston Athey

My goal is to give people the special advantages of small-company investing—the fact that these companies are more vibrant in our economy—but to do it in a fund that has a lower volatility. So that when the inevitable comes and the stocks do go down in some year, they won't go down so far as to trigger people's unhappiness point. They're more likely to stay the course, stay in the stock, stay in the fund, and over the long term do very well for themselves.

Q. Preston, when I first heard about undervalued small companies, I was a little confused: How can a small company be undervalued? And someone explained to me that a lot of small companies that are undervalued were once medium-sized companies and they've fallen down . . . because something bad happened. What percentage of the companies that you buy have experienced problems, as opposed to companies that just are undiscovered?

A. I couldn't tell you the percentage. It might be a quarter of those in the fund. It would be ones that had clearly seen better days in the past with a higher stock price, had come to the point where there were some problems that occurred, and the stocks fell as a result and brought them into a range that you and I might call both small cap and value.

Q. How much of a person's investment portfolio would you suggest that someone have in small-company stocks? Apparently, the conventional wisdom is about 30%.

A. I think that's a question that each individual investor has to examine on his or her own. And I think it's a cliché to talk about risk tolerance and one's ability to absorb risk. I think, over the very long term, this sector of the market will do somewhat better than, say, the general stock market as represented by the Dow Jones industrials or the S&P 500. But as I mentioned earlier, it's very likely that long-term return or long-term performance will be accompanied with higher volatility.

If you're a young person in a secure job with a very long-term investment future, I think 30% is a good number, maybe even 40%. If you're an older person or someone who's not used to investing in the stock market, and you know your own philosophical view of life tends to be quite conservative, then this is an area in which I would own quite a bit less than 30%, maybe just enough to dabble in it and have an investment. But probably you'd be better off being in the bigger, safer, blue chip stocks.

Q. Might someone buy shares of your fund and also buy a small-company growth fund, like New Horizons or T. Rowe Price OTC?

A. Yes, you could do that. And the advantage of doing that is that by spreading the investment among two or three small-company funds, you're very likely to receive the complete benefits of small-company investing without, perhaps, having picked one fund that might go into a dry spell for a year or two and not provide the same returns. So I think that's actually quite a good way to invest.

Q. What are the biggest dangers when you buy small companies? Is it the threat of competition? That a small company will find a niche, then a big company will come along and drive it out of business?

A. Interestingly, no, that's not the biggest threat. Most of the companies that we buy are already pretty well established within their niches, and because they're smaller and more nimble, they can often see the big companies coming and can take steps ahead of time to avoid getting hit by a major product cycle or change in the competitive threat.

What's more likely to happen in a small company is that there will be a change in top management, or an inevitable hiccup in the progress of the company will be magnified by the fact that it may only be a one-product or one-service company. Or it may be located, say, in one geographic area. So, for example, if you're a motel company headquartered in Texas and we have an energy recession, New England might be doing very well, but your company will do poorly because no one will be traveling in Texas.

And that's the sort of thing I think is more likely to happen to a small company.

CHAPTER 30

Dodge & Cox's John A. Gunn: "Among Mutual Funds, We're a Strange Beast."

John A. Gunn, chief investment officer of the Dodge & Cox funds, and his co-managers make decisions as if they must live with them for three or four years. This long-term approach is appropriate: Its Balanced Fund has been around since 1931. And the fund has been rewarded with a steady-as-a-rock long-term performance.

Q. How are the Dodge & Cox funds different from other funds?
A. Among mutual funds, we're a strange beast. One writer has even said that Dodge & Cox isn't in the mutual fund business—which is why he likes us. What he meant was that we don't advertise or bend over backward to publicize ourselves; we're not in the distribution business.

It's true that we're different. We don't want to have phalanxes of people. A friend of mine works for another mutual fund, which has twice the assets we have and 1,200 employees. We have a little over 60 employees, and we don't want or need 1,200. We don't even have any new funds on the horizon, beyond the three we have now.

We're in the investment business, concentrating on stocks and bonds to buy and trying to keep our costs low.

Our three mutual funds are Dodge & Cox Stock, Balanced, and Income. If you buy the Stock Fund and the Income Fund, you would just about have the Balanced Fund. We don't vary the asset allocations in the balanced fund dramatically. Usually we're around 56% in stocks, 38% in bonds. The most we've been in stocks was about 70%, and we're pretty close to the lower end right now. The most we can have in stocks is 75%.

But every once in a while there's a fat pitch, a really good opportunity to load up on stocks or bonds. Maybe every five years or so. Early in 1987, before the Crash, was a great time to load up on bonds when long rates were going up, and so was the stock market—temporarily. So, even though most of the time we might not be doing much with our asset allocation, we have to stay awake.

Our stocks have done well, I think, because of our strong, extensive research and our determination to understand each investment as best we can. We're trying to buy bargains and be well informed about those bargains. Then there's our long-term orientation. And our low turnover. Also, our employees are active investors in the company. We eat our own cooking. All of our pension and profit-sharing plans are invested in the three funds.

Our team approach is another advantage. Everyone here started out at or near the beginning of their business careers, and everyone shares the same general investment philosophy. We're on the same wavelength, even though some of us have different camera angles. All of us are even on one floor, so we can meet quickly.

We try to avoid stocks that in three or four years will be known as value stocks and to buy stocks that we hope someday will be known as growth stocks—unpopular to not-very-popular stocks, with low-to-average expectations of profits. We're not knee-jerk contrarians, but we're always going to be looking at stocks whose prices are dropping. Of course, if a stock is selling at the low end of its historic valuation, it's not that everyone else sees worries and we see nothing but blue skies. The worries are there. But a lot of times they get overdone. And we may also see chances of good surprises.

We screen for a number of things—low price-earnings ratios, low market capitalization to sales, etc. But not low price-book value: That has become less meaningful with share repurchases and large write-offs of retiree medical benefits. There have been a lot of distortions of book value.

Naturally, we're bottom-up investors, just looking for good stocks. We feel that the best top-down strategies come from bottom-up observations. Our 11 research analysts are constantly visiting companies.

We have about the same weighting in technology as the index, but we tend to buy the faster-growing, smaller companies—the ones not written about in *Fortune* and *Business Week*—instead of Intel and MicroSoft and Oracle.

Our bonds tend to be high quality. But we try to boost our yield by buying undervalued issues, such as mortgages. Normally, we're a little light on Treasuries compared with the indexes, because we want the greater yield of corporate bonds. Even so, our average credit quality is high, at AA+. But we do a lot of credit analysis, involving our stock people, too. And we may shorten maturities when we think interest rates might rise. Normally, though, we keep our maturities long, to pick up extra yield.

We make all our decisions—on asset allocation, which stocks or bonds to buy—thinking that these decisions might be frozen for three or four years. That keeps us focused on long-term strategies.

The Balanced fund has grown rapidly of late, but it's no problem because we've always bought big companies and always managed large amounts of money. There's $2.5 billion in our funds, but we manage $12.5 billion in private money.

One more advantage our funds have that I should mention is that we're enormously persistent. We won't sell anything just because it has gone down on us. But we will look at it very carefully, and we'll ask ourselves, "Would we buy it again today?"

CHAPTER 31

PIMCO's Bill Gross: "You *Can* Beat the House."

When Bill Gross was a wee lad growing up in California, he decided to bop down to the gaming tables in Las Vegas and try his hand at blackjack. He was, after all, pretty good at math.

He didn't consider it gambling. It was investing. He knew that he was a good card-counter, and if you can remember which cards have already been played, you can calculate whether the odds on the next throw favor you or the house.

Bill's grubstake was $200. "I just wanted to turn it into something better," he says.

He was rather determined. He played for four months. Sixteen hours a day. Seven days a week. One hundred and twenty days in a row.

"I never took a break," he recalls. "I just played blackjack. I never met anybody, in terms of friendships."

What did the $200 turn into? A tinge of amusement entered his voice: "$9,500."

But... "After I calculated all the hours I had played, it worked out to $4.50 an hour. A little better than minimum wage at the time!"

Still, "It wasn't the money I made, but the lesson I learned, that was valuable." The lesson was: You *can* beat the house.

"The principle stayed with me ever since," he says. "If you use intelligence, or hard work, or a combination of the two, and you play a long enough period of time, you can put the odds in your favor in any market—stocks, bonds, real estate, whatever—and you'll probably come out a winner.

So, when he graduated from college (Duke) and graduate school (UCLA Graduate School of Business), he became an investor in the financial markets . . .

In a recent survey of money managers by *Pensions and Investments* magazine, William H. Gross was identified by his peers as the single most influential authority on the bond market in the country.

He is a founder and the managing director of the Pacific Investment Management Co. (PIMCO), and oversees $70 billion of bond assets, over 1% of such money in the United States.

Morningstar, the mutual fund tracker, has referred to Gross' "uncanny ability to call interest rates."

A slight, soft-spoken gentleman, Gross is an entertaining speaker. Not long ago, he was reminiscing about buying a vanity license plate for his car when he was starting his career. He wanted to impress his bosses, so his license plate said: BONDS.

He drove that car around for a long time, but the license plate elicited only one inquiry. Someone came over and asked, diffidently, "Can you get me . . . a bail bond?"

On his own investments: He's mostly in stocks, and in foreign stocks to boot—Asia and emerging markets. He owns a lot of Harbor International, run by Hakan Castegren. "I'm still pretty young, pushing 52, and I think that equities over the long term are the best investment. Bonds are for older, conservative investors who need income."

On bond versus stock managers: "Bond managers are considered the ghouls of the investment business, coming out at night, going to sleep in the day when the sun comes out. But they don't necessarily want everyone to suffer. They're just terrified of inflation."

Advice for ordinary investors: "Older, conservative investors might boost their yields without sacrificing quality by moving into good mortgage funds—with low expenses and no sales charges."

CHAPTER 32

Twentieth Century's Glenn Fogle: "Comparing Other Funds with Giftrust Is Like Comparing Basketball Players to Michael Jordan."

Glenn Fogle, one of the managers of Twentieth Century Giftrust, has been with the company since 1990. He is a Chartered Financial Analyst and received a B.A. and M.B.A. from Texas Christian University.

Q. Why has Twentieth Century Giftrust done so remarkably well?

A. I think there are a couple of things that deserve credit. The first is that we have a very clear philosophy to follow: to own companies that are showing accelerated earnings growth. And we don't compromise that. That philosophy sometimes is in favor and sometimes is out of favor, but we stick to what we do well, and we don't try to chase fads.

We also benefit at Giftrust, frankly, from the fact that it is rather difficult to put money in. You have to be giving it away. And we haven't been flooded with money chasing our good performance. So the fact that it's been able to stay small has allowed us to concentrate on small cap stocks that are below the radar screen of a lot of the bigger institutional investors.

Q. Can you describe how Giftrust works? You have to make an irrevocable gift to somebody?

A. That's right. It can be a gift to an individual or to a charitable fund. It can be basically to anyone other than your spouse. The trust must have a life of at least 10 years. If it's given to minor children, those minors have to be at the age of majority in the state where they live, 18 or 21, before they can receive the assets of the trust. It has to be the minimum of 10 years. But if it's given to a 5-year-old child, for instance, that minimum might be longer than 10 years.

Q. Can you keep the money in Giftrust after 10 years?

A. Yes. Once the recipients receive the proceeds of the trust, they may choose to leave them in trust. And then it becomes the beneficiary's option as to when to cash out.

Q. But if you gave the money to a 15-year-old, and the 15-year-old was in a state where you reach legal maturity at 21, at 21 you still couldn't get the money.

A. That's right. He'd have to wait at least until he was 25 in that case.

Q. And you cannot make a gift to a spouse.

A. That's correct.

Q. And the minimum first investment, I think, is $500.

A. That's correct. And once the trust is set up, the donor can continue to contribute $50 a month or $100 a month or whatever at periodic intervals without affecting the maturity of the trust.

Q. It's obviously a good idea for someone who is saving for a child's education to consider a fund like 20th Century Giftrust. Would you recommend that someone put all of a college savings fund into Twentieth Century Giftrust? Say, when a child is a year old, should a parent start saving just through Giftrust?

A. I guess I'm from the old-fashioned school that says don't put all your eggs in one basket. Giftrust can be an important part of a plan like that, but I think it also makes sense to have some money set aside in a little more conservative vehicle—and maybe not even in a trust.

Q. That was the answer I was hoping for. Giftrust—while it's a wonderful fund—can be very volatile. And if someone's not accustomed to volatility in the stock market, he might get a little scared by Giftrust.

A. That's true. And one of the things that we stress in relation to Giftrust is that it is a 10-year minimum, and that forces people to look out 10 years into the future. As you know, anyone who has a shorter time horizon, anyone with a one- or two-year time horizon for their money, ought to be in a very conservative investment.

Q. The Twentieth Century funds are famous for buying growing companies, but very few have done as well as Giftrust. In fact, none has done as well as Giftrust. And some have not done well at all. I'm thinking of Twentieth Century Select. Why have these other funds lagged behind? Conventional wisdom is that these funds grew so large that they couldn't buy smaller companies. Does this accord with your viewpoint?

A. That may be part of it. There's actually more to it than that. First of all, in defense of Select, its record until about five years ago was sterling. Through the 70s and early 80s, it was one of the most top-performing funds in America. So we have to ask what's happened in the last five years.

And one of the big changes in the market has been the emergence of technology as a leader. Most tech stocks do not pay dividends; they reinvest their earnings. And Select has a requirement that every security it owns has to pay a dividend. That requirement goes back, I believe, to the 50s. And at that point, it was common for dividends to separate the safe stocks from the risky ones.

Today that may be a bit of a disservice.

Q. You also work with Vista, which hasn't done quite so well as Giftrust. It hasn't done that badly, but it has lagged behind. I guess this is because it buys larger companies, it buys mid-cap stocks?

A. You're accurate on the difference between the funds. Actually, it's kind of tough to compare any fund against Giftrust because that's like comparing any basketball player to Michael Jordan. Compared to its peers, Vista has done adequately. We're not satisfied with the performance, but we've been improving it.

Q. Twentieth Century funds were famous for many years for having no minimum. And I remember Jim Stowers' telling me that somebody once sent in a quarter and he bought shares in one of the Twentieth Century funds. So I guess what happened was all that the paperwork, having very tiny accounts, was getting burdensome to the current investors. So you've now raised your minimum to $1,000 on your funds, for most of your funds. [James Stowers founded the Twentieth Century funds.]

A. That's right.

Q. But I understand that you can invest less than $1,000 if by the end of a year you have $1,000 in a fund.

A. Actually, the way we currently express the rule is you can open an account with any amount of money, but if it's less than $1,000, you have to put in $50 per month on an automatic monthly investment program, something that's taken directly out of your bank account or paycheck and deposited in the funds.

The difference is we're trying to help savers become investors. Someone who puts $100 in a mutual fund and then lets it sit there is a saver. And that type of person ought to be in a bank savings account.

Q. I've always been struck by the fact that Twentieth Century Funds seem to be a very ethical family. Jim Stowers once told me that the funds wanted a low minimum because they want everyone to be able to participate. I once asked him if he was ever tempted to sell stocks short. And he said of course he is; everyone at Twentieth Century was: When you see a stock start slipping, it's very tempting to bet against it. But he said that they felt at Twentieth Century that it was somehow un-American to sell a stock short. What do you think of that?

A. I've heard that story passed around up here, and I think it pretty well illustrates the way that Mr. Stowers looks at the market. He is the most positive and upbeat person you could imagine. And ethics play a very fundamental role around here.

When people are talking about trusting their money to complete strangers, you want to at least have confidence that those people are ethical and trustworthy.

CHAPTER

T. Rowe Price's Chip Morris: "When the Death of the Computer Industry Is Announced, Double Up."

Over the past five years, technology stocks have been sizzling. And no wonder. Technology has been transforming our lives. Think how different the world has become thanks to cellular phones, smart automobiles, software that does your taxes, and so forth. Thanks to the VCR, for example, I have managed to watch every lousy movie made in the last 20 or 25 years.

T. Rowe Price Science and Technology Fund is unusual in that it's far more diversified than most technology sector funds. What other technology fund invests in pharmaceuticals, chemicals, and waste management?

Here are excerpts from an interview with Charles (Chip) A. Morris, who runs the fund and whose nickname, I am relieved to report, predated his interest in microchip companies. Morris is a Chartered Financial Analyst, having received his B.S. degree from Indiana University and his M.B.A. from Stanford. He joined T. Rowe Price in 1987.

Q. Why are you optimistic about technology?

A. Wherever you look, technology is becoming increasingly pervasive in our everyday lives, and this trend is accelerating.

My parents never used a computer. I first used a computer when I was in college. My nephew is using a computer, and he's in the third grade. So, if we've got grade-school kids using computers, and cell phones becoming common for the Generation X—of which I'm a member—you can imagine what's going to happen in 20 years.

So there is a reallocation of our disposable income that is going toward technology in one way or another, whether in products we buy, like software; or embedded in products we buy, like automobiles and elevators. This has broad implications: The consumer market is much broader and deeper than the corporate market.

Q. Is technology a cyclical area?

A. Typically you can depend on the winter as a good period for technology stocks and the summer as a poor period. But in any one year, you can't depend on it. So the best thing for investors to do is dollar-cost average into the fund.

We advocate that our investors be patient, give us three to five years. Don't panic—or get euphoric. Kind of just stay the course. Or, when things are flying high, they should take some money off the table. And when the death of the computer industry is announced on the front page of the *Washington Post*—double up.

Q. What worries you?

A. I worry about (1) how the PC sector will do—all it has to do, though, is be OK; (2) a worldwide economic contraction; and (3) the fact that five years ago you couldn't convince a [diversified] portfolio manager to own technology stocks. They could be down 40% in a day. They were easier to ignore. Today, technology is much more widely owned. I worry about portfolio managers—who don't have a lot of experience investing in technology—becoming panicky and selling out.

CHAPTER 34

Janus' James P. Craig: "When You Get Stubborn, You Get into Trouble."

Born in 1956 in Decatur, Alabama, Craig studied business at the University of Alabama, and received an M.B.A. in Finance from Wharton in 1981. He spent two years as an investment analyst with Trust Company of the West.

Q. What is your investment strategy? What makes your style different from other managers' styles?

A. A disciplined focus on earnings acceleration to the exclusion of macro-theories or forecasts. That's not a lot different than a lot of people. It's the intensity of the discipline, the focus on accelerating earnings that draws our stock picks, and the way we approach running the money on an individual stock-by-stock basis.

Forecasting the economy and interest rates is interesting but not very profitable because no one can really do it. So it's our intent to only invest where there is accelerating earnings momentum, and the unique thing about us versus a lot of other people is if I cannot find the issues, then I don't invest, even if it requires my carrying a high cash position in a rising market. So I would rather carry the cash than invest in something I wasn't fervently excited about. If we don't find good value, or we don't find those opportunities, we'll carry cash.

So it's not uncommon for the Janus Fund to be 30% plus in cash, even in a market I would characterize as a good market. Most people in my business would take that 30% cash and buy something, just to be exposed to the market that they thought was good. I won't do that. I'd rather carry the cash than buy then, and only invest in those opportunities that I feel, you know, really good about. And sometimes that hurts, but over the period of time that I've been in the business it's been a strength, the backbone of our performance, because that keeps me from getting involved in marginal situations that I don't know a lot about.

So it's just a focus on the best opportunities, and the willingness to carry cash, which differentiates us from a lot of other people. A lot of people would look at 30% cash as a bet against the market.

To my mind, it's nothing of the sort. Even with that much cash, I should beat the market on the upside because my stock picks should do that much better. And Marsico's strategy is pretty similar.

We spend all of our time modeling the earnings of companies, trying to move out two years in earnings estimates, and where we find a discrepancy between our earnings projections and Wall Street, we get aggressive.

Q. Do you also do in-the-field research, as he does?

A. Yes, I do. We both are active. We are active analysts. We have a staff of analysts working with us. Now, I don't do every one of my companies; that would be impossible.

But there are many companies that I am exclusively the quote-unquote "analyst" on here at the shop, particularly a lot of the insurance companies. I do those. And some of the small ones. But you know, we are portfolio managers, and we do manage portfolios, but we are analysts as well.

Our focus is on the estimating of earnings and not sitting back and theorizing about, you know, Germany and interest rates, currencies and politics, and stuff.

It's interesting; that's what a lot of people in my business do, but I don't see how they ever make any money at it because no one really knows.

Q. Does anything about your investment style reflect your personality?

A. I have a very keen willingness to accept my mistakes and correct them and go on. I'm not stubborn. That trait in a person is very detrimental in my business. When you get stubborn, you get into trouble. So if there's any one aspect of my personality, it is that I am not a stubborn person, and that helps me a great deal. And I am willing to admit my mistakes very quickly.

Q. When I talked to Thomas Marsico, he emphasized how important good research is.

A. Oh, yes. We make mistakes, and I'm quick to correct those, but the key is getting an edge. There's a lot of publicly available information, but calling suppliers and customers and detecting trends early, earlier than maybe even the managements of the companies do, that's what gives us the excess returns over the market, that's our value added. That's what we're paid for, that's what we spend our time doing. And a lot of it's not very glamorous; a lot of it's grunt work, to be honest. But that information-gathering process is what gives us the edge on the market.

Q. It's got to be hard to be able to sort out who is reliable.

A. Oh, yes, it is; a lot of times management will mislead you, sometimes on purpose, sometimes unwittingly. But you can't just rely on the management of a company for your information.

Q. What do you think about market-timing?

A. I don't think you can really predict the market on a short-term basis to any probable degree. Someone may be able to once in a while catch it right, but over a long period of time, there are just too many psychological factors that are too hard to really quantify and pin down, and without that quantification, you really can't be consistent.

Q. If you consider the market worrisome, would you then go toward more conservative stocks?

A. No, I go for those stocks where I found a change in the earnings patterns of the company, and I don't classify stocks as being aggressive or defensive necessarily. It's how much confidence I have in our estimation. In our portfolio I expect that some companies I just know dead to rights are going to report this kind of earnings number. Some others, there are a few questions, OK? I classify those companies as safe bets, but the safe bet may be the most aggressive stock to somebody else; do you see what I mean?

So, no, I don't classify, I don't move assets around like that. I look for unknown earnings movements, basically. And that's where I add value. And essentially that's really all I can do to be paid, instead of indexing your portfolio, which people can do very cheaply. They pay us to do something.

Q. Do you agree with the statement, "The hardest part of investing is knowing when to sell"?

A. No. That's not the hardest part. To a lot of people it is, but to me, it's pretty simple. I sell them when the multiple on earnings gets ahead of the growth rate by a significant amount, or when I have made a mistake in analyzing the business trends, or something fundamental changes in the business, then that's a very easy decision.

You know, we have a drug stock and they introduce a new product and the product doesn't sell as well as we expected, that's not a hard decision, that's an easy decision.

Q. Do you have any kind of stop-loss system, even if it's only kept in your own head?

A. Basically, if I buy a stock, if it falls over 20% I have to assume the stock knows something I don't, OK? And I will cut a part of the position by discipline on that basis. If I paid $30 for something, and all of a sudden in short order it's twenty-three bucks, I will sell some of it, maybe 20% or 25%t of the position, because my experience is that I missed something. OK, I do not like to average down. I like the stocks I own to go up. And if they're going down, then I have to think that I made a mistake in my analysis or something, and that's usually the case.

Q. How many funds do you think the average person should own?

A. OK, besides common stocks, municipals, and all that, I think they should probably have exposure to at least two fund families, and within those fund families, probably a total of three or four funds. I know that's kind of specific, but they should diversify among at least two fund families. I mean, my marketing people would be on me for saying that because "one-stop shopping and put all your assets here; we've got plenty of funds for you." But if you came to me outside the business and I just told you what I would like to see you do, you should diversify to at least two groups, two types of management, two styles, two sets of people, and then within those groups you should have a couple of funds, depending on how aggressive you want to be.

What you used to have to do was go to a stockbroker. He took 7% of your money and then put you into something that may or may not work.

Q. And then they want you to constantly sell or buy so that they get commissions back and forth.

A. That's right. I mean our expenses are like nine-tenths of 1%, and we've proven our performance, the whole industry has—there's no commission up front, no commission taken out, what you see is what you get, it's cheap, and it's been good, and it's diversified. You're buying into a pool of 40 or 50 stocks, as opposed to buying one stock that could do all kinds of things. So it's really a good product, and it's been reflected in the growth of the industry. We're killing retail brokers.

Q. Are there any investors whom you personally admire?

A. Oh, yeah. Well, I admire George Soros and Warren Buffett.

Q. And do you know either one of them personally?

A. No.

Q. Do you have any general advice to give investors?

A. Yes, and this is as far as equities go. You have to understand the risk involved in equity investing, you have to be able to have your investment in these equity funds for a period of years. You cannot expect to go in and use equity funds to make short-term profits. You have to give us a chance to earn the returns over a whole period of time.

What happens to a lot of people is they come in at the top, the market goes down, they lose 4% or 5%, they take their money out, then the market comes back, and they're not there. They don't try to time it, but that's essentially what they're doing. And they just can't do it, because they have busy lives and they do other things for a living. Give us the money and give us the time to earn the returns. But in equities, it has to be money that you're going to hold for a period of years because it is volatile.

I don't think you should have 75-, 80-year-old people putting their retirement nest egg that they live off of into the equity market. They need to be in income markets. They just have to understand the risk of equities and give us some time.

Q. Which investment books, if any, do you recommend?

A. I don't know that many. But I will tell you, for a professional investor, the one book I got the most out of was a book called *Reminiscences of a Stock Operator,* which is still in print. It's a book that was written in the 20s, and it's a book written by a person named Jesse Livermore. It was very good. As far as for individuals, Peter Lynch's book *One Up on Wall Street* is very good, and *The Money Game* by Adam Smith is very good.

Q. How did you get interested in mutual funds?

A. Well, I got interested in the business of pension management when I was in college. I loved the stock market; it was a very fast-growing area because in the 70s, 1973, the ERISA law was passed which required employers to put dollars up to back retirement benefits. Somebody had to manage that money in the bond market and the stock market, and so it created an industry, and the industry was exploding in the late 70s, and that's why I was attracted to that industry. From there, I got involved in mutual funds and moved here to Janus in 1983, basically because I wanted to do small companies, and they were going to form a mutual fund for me to do that, so that's why I came here. And it's been great.

It's pretty casual here, and we try to keep doors open; you know, anyone can walk in.

It's good for information flow. You get into these stilted office environments—you have to have meetings, schedule meetings and all that, and you get political about it, and it doesn't work. Here it's wide open, and we try to keep it that way.

CHAPTER 35

Janus 20's Thomas F. Marsico: "An Intuitive Nature Is a Big Plus."

Born in Denver in 1955, Marsico studied biology at the University of Colorado and finance at the University of Denver. He spent three years as a senior portfolio manager with Fred Alger Management and three and a half years as an analyst with Boettcher & Company. He was named Morningstar's 1989 Portfolio Manager of the Year for his guidance of the Janus 20 Fund.

Q. The Janus 20 Fund takes its name from the two-faced Roman god of gates and doorways, signifying new beginnings?

A. The name also refers to the god's ability to look both forwards and backwards, where one has gone before and where one will be going, where one was previously and where one will be in the future.

Q. What is the keynote of your investment strategy?

A. The most important ingredient in our strategy is our emphasis on research. We really strive to know and understand our companies. We've carefully built a team of perceptive, well-rounded researchers. They have degrees in history, biology, English; they are educationally well-rounded, perceptive, curious. They are able to ask the right questions, which is an advantage in investigating trends and markets. There is a degree of intuitiveness necessary—an intuitive/perceptive nature is a big plus. We need to be able to go where the perceptions are moving.

I'm very fortunate to have a great research team. I was able to bring many of them with me from New York when I came out here [to Denver], and we've grown together.

Q. Do you get involved in any of the research personally?

A. Oh, yes! I don't just direct the research team—I go right out into the areas, stores, businesses myself. I'll visit an area where they are testing/trying something new to see how it works or doesn't work; I'll check out these new business ideas. I recently returned from Tampa, Florida, where a fast-food chain is experimenting with dual drive-ins.

Q. So you go and check out if the dual drive-in actually is an asset—you'll drive through yourself and watch others?

A. Exactly. You have to be out there to see what's really happening, that goes for any business, retail, anything.

Q. So you have a truly hands-on research methodology.

A. You have to combine the on-paper research with field work to get the full scope of a situation. If you look at a company just on paper, you can be misled. A company can look great, but there are other factors which come into play which can show a company is in trouble—factors that have to be picked up off-paper. In our current global market, it's important to stay in touch with the macro-environment.

Q. The tumbling of Europe, the [dissolution of] Soviet Union—all the political upheaval and restructuring?

A. That's part of it, but also something like the current eruptions of Mt. Pinatubo, which will affect the world's weather—that's a macro-environmental factor that will have an effect on certain companies.

Q. To switch to another direction ... which personality traits or qualities do you think distinguish a successful investor from an unsuccessful investor? Do you think a Type A or Type B personality is better?

A. You have to be comfortable enough with yourself, to be willing to immediately admit you've made a mistake, and to be able to have the confidence to disagree with something even if the majority opinion is at odds with your perception or conclusion. If you can admit a mistake early, then you can correct it sooner. As for Type A versus Type B—there's no stereotype, I know all kinds of equally successful personalities. A negative would be someone impulsive or inpatient. Logic and self-discipline are helpful.

I have a degree in biology and have found that to be very helpful, the emphasis on thinking things out logically.

Q. You've described the importance of good research. Do you rely on outside brokers as well?

A. We use outside brokers to a very minor extent. We may get some ideas that way, but we would use our team to evolve them and to put them across in our way.

Q. Do you use any form of market-timing?

A. No, we don't use market-timing, although I do have some sort of internal clock which responds. I believe in economic cycles, but right now our country's heavy debt levels show we'll be in a very, very slow growth cycle—the global economy as well will slow the magnitude of any upswing. We won't see the volatile upswings we've seen in the past. You won't see the big dips or big rises. It will be basically a slow, consistent 2% growth for a while.

Q. If you couldn't find good stocks, would you invest more in cash or in other vehicles?

A. Cash is okay, but I would avoid areas I didn't have expertise in.

Q. If you perceived the market as worrisome, would you go toward more conservative stocks?

A. I would sell the overvalued stocks and then go to a larger cash position.

Q. Do you agree with the statement, "The hardest part of investing is knowing when to sell"?

A. Knowing when to sell can be the easiest thing to do. Any fundamental change in a company is one obvious sign to sell; any major change in the macro-environment which will particularly affect a certain company is another point toward moving to sell—although at times this can be a more subtle clue to sell, backing up the importance of field work.

Q. What is the hardest part of investing then?

A. Knowing how to balance a portfolio is the hardest part of investing. Ideally you want to have 75 percent of your portfolio performing well. For that you need to get the mix right. The current themes now are banking and finance, but we diversify—we also look to retail and pharmaceutical companies for a balance. You want a good mix.

Q. Do you have a stop-loss system—even if it's only kept in your head?

A. I have an in-head stop order: Any big drop of 15% or more means sell, even if I don't understand at the time what is happening, what the contributing factors are. I have to go by the performance of the company. Obviously the numbers are telling me something and I have to act!

Q. I recently read an article saying that lower-end retailers like Wal-Mart should not be recommended, that they are overpriced and will level out in earnings. But one could argue that the lower-end retailers will grow, especially if the economy stays sluggish.

A. More and more people are shopping smart. People realize they don't have to go to big-name department stores to get quality at decent, affordable prices. The lower end has improved; Wal-Mart will continue to be a good buy.

Q. How many funds do you think the average investor should own?

A. Of course it all depends on their age, lifestyle, family status, etc., which can vary greatly. But the average investor should generally have three or four funds.

Q. Are there any investors whom you personally admire?

A. Yes . . . Tom Bailey—who launched the Janus Funds— and Warren Buffett.

Q. Which investment books would you recommend?

A. Peter Lynch's *One Up on Wall Street*.

Q. Do you have any advice you would like to pass to investors in general?

A. Well, what my Dad always told me . . . be like the tortoise and take the long-term, steady approach and don't invest in the latest fad.

CHAPTER 36

Vanguard's Ian MacKinnon: "We Search Avidly for the Free Lunch."

Ian A. MacKinnon, senior vice-president and head of the fixed-income group at the Vanguard Group, was born in 1948. He received a B.A. from Lafayette College in 1970 and an M.B.A. in Finance from Penn State.

Q. How do you keep your costs down? Not by paying your people less, I hope?

A. No, the employees at Vanguard are well paid. But the corporate structure at Vanguard is unique in the mutual fund business. Vanguard is truly the only mutual fund company where the operating company itself is owned by the funds, which are themselves owned by the shareholders.

What that means is that the normal profit margin that is siphoned off by the owners of the operating company is returned dollar for dollar to the owners of the fund, the shareholders.

Q. I see.

A. And that profit margin is substantial. If you look at a Dreyfus or a Franklin or a T. Rowe Price, the owners of the operating company are the stockholders. The stock is traded on the New York Exchange, and their earnings margins are really quite fantastic.

Vanguard knows we generate the same kind of earnings, but they return dollar for dollar to the shareholders—in terms of higher yields and higher dividends.

Q. I see.

A. That differential is easily a half to a full percentage point per year in annual returns. It really is substantial.

Q. Another familiar question I have for you is: Are interest rates predictable? Or are they predictable only at certain times?

A. I would say the latter. In general, interest rates are unpredictable. Occasionally they are predictable.

Q. At extreme points?

A. Yes, exactly. And we tend to hew to that particular religious skepticism. Our style of management is one of not betting a lot on the direction of interest rates, and not betting very often on the direction of interest rates. Although we do at extreme times have strong opinions and do change the price sensitivity of our portfolios, we don't do it that often—and we do it under controlled circumstances. I think the result is that we don't lose a lot of money guessing wrong on the direction of rates. And occasionally we make a decent amount of money guessing correctly.

Q. How else do you add value besides your being economical and your occasionally guessing the direction of interest rates?

A. We focus our attention on a style of management that's fairly well established in the equity markets, and—it's no secret—it's called value investing.

But for a bond portfolio, rather than looking at a specific issue that is cheap relative to another issue, we tend more to look at kinds of issues—sectors of the market that are cheap relative to something else.

We even look at—this gets kind of abstruse—the structural characteristics of securities. In the case of a bond, we examine not only the coupon and the maturity but also the embedded call features of the security [call features: whether bonds can be redeemed early by their issuers]. And we try to establish whether those structural characteristics are fairly valued or not, and if our analysis indicates that they're unfairly valued, we would move out of securities with the rich characteristics and move into securities with the cheap characteristics. That might mean buying a whole slug of discount bonds rather than premium bonds [bonds whose market prices have sunk rather than bonds whose prices have climbed]. It might mean buying noncallable bonds rather than bonds with slightly higher yields that happen to be callable. In fact, that's been a very fundamental cornerstone of our success over the last 5 to 10 years—placing a great deal of emphasis on bonds that are resistant to early calls.

Q. That's in line with your thinking that interest rates were going down. [Typically bonds are redeemed early when interest rates have fallen.]

A. Partly that, and partly that the callability of the bonds that we were buying, or could potentially buy, was not giving us a sufficient extra yield. Over the last several years, the yield differential between callable and noncallable bonds has been so small that it wasn't worth that modest incremental yield to accept the risk of the bonds being called away from us prematurely. So again, it was a value decision, and it's paid off quite handsomely for us.

Another thing that we do is that we try to search avidly for the free lunch. The free lunch in some cases is the arbitrage opportunities between the interest market and the cash market.

What we do is—on a purely risk-control basis—we might go long in cash bonds and short a futures contract, or reverse that process and go long a futures contract and sell the cash bonds. Either way, we're identifying that one is rich or cheap relative to the other, and we're trying to milk the convergence of those two securities back to their historic average relationship.

Q. A form of arbitrage.

A. Right. It's not dissimilar to stock arbitrage, the index arbitrage that takes place among arbitrageurs with the S&P 500 interest contract. There happens to be a similar contract in the municipal market, on the Bond Buyer Index 40 futures contract.

Q. I see. Another question: Are people who are good at investing in bonds also good at investing in stocks, or is there a different psychology required?

A. I think there is a significantly different psychology required. In a stock portfolio, a great deal of the returns available are derived from the selection of individual securities. And a lot of the differences in relative returns result from your being a better stock-picker than your competitors. In a bond fund, there's rarely that much of a difference between Bond A and Bond B if they have similar characteristics, i.e., similar coupons, average quality, average maturity.

Q. I see.

A. So that's what makes a good bond manager—not so much that he picks better bonds, although there is some element of that—but that he picks bonds that have superior performing characteristics. So the successful bond fund manager tends to look less at Issue A or Issue B as much as he's looking at Structure A versus Structure B.

Q. Does that require different personality attributes? I think of equity managers as being quick thinking and independent thinking, and going against the grain.

A. Contrarian, you mean?

Q. Yes.

A. Well, I think you get contrarian bond managers. I think there are similarities in that regard, but I think that bond managers tend to be more long-term oriented than stock managers. It takes longer for a successful scenario to unfold in the bond markets, typically.

Q. Would you say that successful fixed-income managers are more patient, or inclined to be patient?

A. Yes, I would say that. There are similarities to value investors. I know that value investors among stocks tend to have avocations that are kind of reflective of their whole style of managing money. I think value bond investors have avocations that are similar. I happen to be a wine collector myself.

Q. You're patiently waiting for it to age?

A. Well, not only that, but I don't believe in just paying anything for a bottle of wine. I have a very, very avid and personal economic interest in making sure that the wines that I buy not only are good-tasting but represent good value.

Q. Are there any other avocations like that, that you find among value?

A. Well, I know that John Neff [formerly of Vanguard/Windsor], for instance, likes to buy all of his clothing at the discount outlets. And I think that that is emblematic of his contrarian search for good value among the forgotten or the underappreciated or the despised of equity markets. I think that he carries that out into his personal life. Doesn't like to pay up for anything, and I don't like to pay up for anything, either.

CHAPTER 36   Vanguard's Ian MacKinnon

Q. Another question I have for you is impossible to answer, but we'll see how you deal with it. Is it better to give a fixed-income manager a lot of rope, saying invest anywhere, invest in Ginnie Maes or junk bonds, or should you give him a narrow focus, saying invest only in short-term bonds? I know it's possible to make arguments for both.

A. You can, and Vanguard's corporate philosophy has gravitated almost without exception to the latter kind of portfolio management mandate, not only on the bond side but on the equity side. And what Vanguard corporately and philosophically is trying to do is to enhance the relative predictability of results, and that means that if you have a Ginnie Mae fund, you invest exclusively in Ginnie Maes and you compare yourself to a Ginnie Mae index. Any variation of your return relative to the index is going to be smaller than a portfolio manager who has a wide-open gamut between Ginnies, corporate bonds, Treasury bonds, short-term, long-term—you see what I'm saying?

Q. Yes.

A. And you can certainly make a case for either one, but there are pluses and minuses, pros and cons. The pros are that a manager with a greater gamut, if he's a gifted and successful manager, can add more value relative to a generic kind of index if he's got more flexibility. The con is that he could lose more value.

Q. Right.

A. And a second drawback is—whether he adds more value or he subtracts value through his activities—he increases the amount of volatility against that benchmark.

Q. OK.

A. Most of the mutual fund industry has moved much more closely to the tightly defined portfolio parameter than the loosely defined portfolio.

Q. I think some shareholders are sometimes unpleasantly surprised to find out that a fund with a generic name is investing in junk bonds.

A. Yes. But you see that less and less because industry observers like Michael Lipper are culling through these kinds of portfolios and no longer putting the generic-type portfolio in a generic category; if they see that it's got over 20% junk, they're now putting it in the junk category, and the industry starts comparing it to the other junk bonds. So you may not have it in the title, but in terms of the way the professionals view things happening—that's now a junk bond fund rather than an investment-grade fund.

Q. Do you think investors who are interested in fixed-income investments should have mutual funds along with individual bonds or just stick with mutual funds?

A. There's no complete answer to that. The issues are ones of professional management and diversity and expenses. Those are the three points on the triangle that determine the advisability of owning individual securities rather than funds. And I guess there's maybe a fourth point—maybe it's not a triangle—and that is whether you're going to need your money at a certain time. If you absolutely need your money at a certain time, like for a child going into college, and you want to fund that with the proceeds of an investment, you can obtain money at the end of that horizon, at the child's matriculation date, or with more certainty if you own actual securities that mature on or around that date. Individual holdings make more sense in that case than a bond fund or a stock fund which has no fixed maturity, although there are kinds of bond funds that do have fixed maturities—they're called unit trusts.

Q. OK.

A. The other points revolve around whether you're able to obtain sufficient diversity to offset the unsystematic risk of a small number of investments. In the case of a bond fund, bond funds in general are very, very broadly diversified, as are stock funds. Bond funds, however, typically are in the millions of dollars, and you need probably a couple of million dollars to adequately diversify an individual portfolio.

Q. Wow.

A. You want to be able to buy round lots of bonds, so you want to buy, let's say, a minimum investment size of $100,000 per holding of bonds. To get up to 20 bonds, you need $2 million. If you try to buy bonds in denominations of less than $100,000, you really start getting chewed up on transaction cost.

Q. Let me ask you also about two other things. One is, how do you feel about competing against your own bond index fund? Say there's an investor out there who wants to go into bonds via mutual funds, and he likes the bond index fund. What percentage should he put into the bond index fund and what percentage should he put into managed funds?

A. You see, our managed funds don't have exactly the same risk exposure as the bond index fund, so it's a little bit of a fish-and-fowl comparison. Our bond index fund has about a 10-year average maturity. Our investment-grade bond portfolio, which has many attributes in common with the bond market fund, has an average maturity of over 20 years. Our short-term corporate portfolio has an average maturity of two and a half years. Our government fund, our long-term Treasury portfolio, has an average maturity of 22 years. Our intermediate Treasury portfolio comes close to the bond market with about an eight-year average maturity—but it consists entirely of Treasuries. So we really don't have anything on a risk basis that is closely comparable to the bond market fund.

If we did, I would relish the opportunity to compete against the index fund because it's such a fair benchmark, and it's a tough benchmark to beat. And if you're able to beat it, you've accomplished quite a bit.

Q. Would you suggest an investor put 50% into the bond market portfolio and 50% into the managed funds, or would it depend upon whether he wanted 10-year bonds or not?

A. Right, you first ask yourself whether he wants bonds at all and what mix of bonds he wants relative to stocks. You sort of get to the broader asset allocation issue first. Once you've decided that a certain percentage of your pool of investments ought to be in fixed-income, that's when you make the decision as to how much risk you're willing to take among your bond investments, and the 10-year area represents some kind of middle ground. It's certainly got more potential risk than short-term portfolios, but it's got substantially less risk than the long-term stuff that Vanguard offers. And if that middle ground is a comfort area, then I think the bond market fund makes a lot of sense.

Q. I have a recommendation for you. I think you should start a fixed-income fund similar to Vanguard STAR. STAR has about 60 or 70 percent stocks in it. You should have a fund of funds that give people a slice of various fixed-income funds—you know, Ginnie Mae funds, junk funds, short-term bonds, long-term bonds. The fact that you have STAR means there's a gap, because you don't have something similar to STAR in the fixed-income area.

A. Well, we do. Bond Market Fund is like STAR, because you've got short-, intermediate-, and long-term bonds in the fund. You've got Ginnie Maes, you've got Treasuries, you've got corporates in there. The only thing that Bond Market Fund doesn't have is junk, and you could maybe create a synthetic STAR bond fund that was part bond market index fund and part high-yield, which would include the junk. But in a real sense, the Bond Market Fund is already STAR-like in its composition.

Q. I was thinking actually of Price Spectrum Income, which not only contains a variety of their fixed-income funds but which is managed in the sense that when they think that one market is a better buy.

A. Well—they shift. They allocate the assets. You've got a point there. It would be possible to create a fund of funds where you shift the allocation where you believe the highest value is, and you're either going to win or lose on an asset-allocation basis. I will say that creating a fund of funds is something that the Securities and Exchange Commission has frowned upon rather intensely over the years because of the potential for abuse.

Q. Fees on fees . . .

A. Right. Dating back to Bernie Cornfeld and Robert Vesco. In that era, there was a lot of abuse. Vanguard has been able to create a fund of funds where there is only one layer of fees deducted, and I believe that T. Rowe Price has followed a similar convention.

Q. Who are your heroes in fixed-income investments? Are there any predecessors who you feel pioneered the field of investing in fixed income?

A. Well, there are some heroes in a couple of different senses. I think that Bill Gross at PIMCO is probably one of the heroes of the bond market, and to my mind a kindred spirit from an investment perspective. I think at the opposite end of the spectrum would be a Van Hoisington. Van Hoisington is one of the last of the great cowboys of bond investing. He tends to be an adrenalin-pumping market-timer who's either a hundred percent long or a hundred percent short. He manages pension money, so he's on the institutional side. But you have to respect that kind of gut-wrenching survivability. He's been able to maintain that kind of investment style over so many years, when interest rates are so notoriously difficult to predict.

I don't happen to believe in his philosophy, don't get me wrong. I look at him the same way that I might look at Joe Granville, one of the market technicians.

Q. How has he done?

A. Well, it depends on the time period that you measure him, but I'd say at certain times he's done spectacularly well and at other times he has crashed and burned. That's what I mean by gut-wrenching, adrenalin-pumping kinds of investment performance.

Q. Why aren't fixed-income managers like Van Hoisington as famous as equity fund managers?

A. Number one, the stock market historically has been much better-performing than the bond market. You look at the long-term trend in interest rates, and I mean really long-term trend in interest rates, up until 1982 the secular trend in rates has been upward for 40 years from the mid-40s to the early 80s. So if you're a bond fund investor, you are fighting the gradual erosion in the prices of your securities that's lasted 30-odd years—obviously interrupted during brief periods by bull markets in bonds. But you don't find any heroes in a 37-year secular bear market. That's for starters.

Since the early 80s, bond funds have received more attention than they had. Since then, the annualized compound rate of return of bond funds has been somewhere in the neighborhood of 13%. And you have produced some bond heroes over that time. But the heroism of those bond investors has been overshadowed by the 17% annualized rate of return available on stocks during the same decade.

That's one reason, and also you've got a few equity managers that have so spectacularly beaten the average return on stocks—the Peter Lynches, the John Neffs periodically. The Mario Gabellis. The Templetons.

Q. One more question. A mistake that ordinary investors make with fixed-income investments is that they look for yield rather than total return. What are the mistakes that sophisticated investors make?

A. I think that sophisticated investors tend to have a higher degree of confidence in their ability to predict interest rates than is warranted. I think that they tend to focus too much on the short term.

Q. You mentioned before that you rarely try and predict interest rates. How often do you think you're right with regard to deciding where interest rates are going?

A. Probably about 80% of the time. But we don't bet that often because, in order for us to develop a strong conviction that rates are going to move in one direction or the other, we need to see a very, very strong body of evidence.

CHAPTER 37

The Yacktman Fund's Donald T. Yacktman: "I'm Eating My Own Cooking."

Born in 1941, Yacktman received a B.S. in Economics at the University of Utah in 1965 and an M.B.A. in Finance from Harvard in 1967. He worked for Stein Roe & Farnham and Continental Bank before becoming portfolio manager of Selected American Shares in Chicago in 1983. He was named Morningstar's manager of the year for 1991. He left Selected American to manage his own fund in 1992.

Q. Is your strategy at The Yacktman Fund the same as it was with Selected American Shares?

A. Yes, I'm still a value investor. Some people consider me more of a blend manager, emphasizing growth as well as value, but that's only because a lot of growth stocks end up as value stocks, and that's when I buy them.

I have a three-part investment strategy, which is why our logo is a triangle: I like good businesses, concerned about their shareholders and selling at bargain prices.

Q. Why have you been so much more successful than other value managers?

A. What separates the men from the boys is that when good stocks go down, the boys don't view them as better buys. They get nervous and get scared out. With me, if lettuce is $1 a head, I don't buy it. If it's two for $1, I buy two. Either you're a good shopper or you're not. Good shoppers look for quality that's on sale. The average stock in the Dow Jones 30 varies in price by 50% in the course of a year. It may go from $30 to $45 or from $45 to $32. We prefer buying stocks at $31 or $32 rather than $42 or $43.

Q. What mistakes have you learned from?

A. This is a humbling business. You could always have done better—always bought cheaper or sold higher. Or you could have sold, and bought it back against cheaper before it went up again. And other people always seem to have done better. What I've learned is to stay with quality, and not pay too much attention to a stock just because it's cheap.

Q. Who is the ideal investor in your fund?

A. People who have long-term, 10-year investment horizons. We should do very well over time, even if not week to week or month to month. We're not high fliers. Our strategy is patience. We're not looking for instant gratification.

Q. Do you market-time at all?

A. No, what we buy isn't determined by the stock market. We do look carefully at prices, though, and if there are no bargains, we leave stocks alone. We've been called market-timers because we had a big cash position in the autumn of 1987 and in 1989, but we're not market-timers.

Q. Why do you want a company to be shareholder-oriented?

A. It's helpful if a manager has his personal wealth tied up in a company. He'll act more like a shareholder. In my own case, all my retirement money is in The Yacktman Fund. So I'm eating my own cooking.

CHAPTER 38

Mutual Series' Michael Price: "All This Nonsense That Wall Street Creates..."

"My biography is very short. I was born in 1951; I went to the University of Oklahoma and graduated in 1973 and came here [the New York area]. There's not much. I've never been an astronaut or a fighter pilot, thank God!"

Q. Would you describe your strategy?
A. Well, we are kind of a long-term investment company. We're categorized as a growth and income fund, which we are. But we really are a special situation fund and a long-term investor. We are bottoms-up investors; we buy companies because of specific reasons. We don't buy stocks because of feelings about the market, or interest rates, or the election, or inflation; we only buy assets at a discount.

We couple that with two other things: bankruptcy investing, which is just a cheaper or more interesting way to buy assets at a discount, and we trade in stocks of companies involved in mergers, tender offers, liquidations, spinoffs. We do those things to get rates of return on our cash.

That's it; that's all. Those are components of the portfolio. We don't have a strategy—it's the wrong word; we have a kind of philosophy of buying assets at a discount, and our approach is by those three things: Graham and Dodd [value] investing, bankruptcies, and deals. That's all we do. We don't really look at other groups.

If the market doesn't reward the value investor, and it didn't in 1990 and 1991, we don't change what we're doing—because we believe in what we're doing.

Q. What do you do differently from other value investors?

A. I don't know, it's how you do the work, having an attitude that you've got to do your own work. You can't just take what others tell you a company or an asset is worth. You have to get several inputs to value assets. You've got to be somewhat disciplined to make sure you wait until the market hands you the stock at a cheap price—it's very hard to do. In other words, do good work on the valuation side and then wait for the market to give it to you cheaply. I think we do very good work on the valuation and on the market side, but sometimes we pay too much on the market, and sometimes we buy things at the right price. We stick to this philosophy. It's great if you can do the homework and then wait for the market to give you things at a big discount from what they are worth, making sure you're right on what they're worth. That's the best philosophy, you know; you don't have to pay attention to technical analysis, or the gibberish on Wall Street, or new product conventions.

Wall Street basically doesn't eat its own cooking. In the last 5 or 10 years—I don't know how long you've been watching Wall Street—but you've had the invention of zero coupon bonds, PIKs, options, futures. They really take what is a very simple mechanism, which is capital formation and capital investment, and make it much more complex than it needs to be, because Wall Street can earn big fees in commissions on the issuance and trading of those instruments. Now sure, for all these guys who want to hedge positions or trade currencies, or hedge shipments of machinery to Germany by buying or selling the mark before you ship the goods. I don't understand that because I'm not in that type of business. But all those things create a lot of noise, a lot of distractions, from what is a very simple business for an investor, which is to buy a stock based on what the business is worth at half of that price.

If they're not there, you don't buy them; if they're there, you buy them and you wait—because sooner or later they're going to trade for what they're worth. All this nonsense Wall Street creates—

CHAPTER 38 Mutual Series' Michael Price

junk bonds, PIKs, zeroes, futures and options, or all the different strategies, all the things you read about in the [Wall Street] *Journal*—they tend to pull investors' attention away from the fundamental things you should pay attention to. What we try to do at Mutual Shares is view the world simply; don't get distracted by all of the stuff Wall Street cooks up. Stick to the simple stuff. Buy oil at below $5 a barrel, and gas for 50 cents, and a dollar for 50 cents. You buy liquid assets as cheap as you can . . . because then you can't lose much money.

We are not stock players, and we're not trying to guess future earnings. We don't come in the morning and say, "Oh, the market is high, let's buy some S&P puts." We just would never do those things.

Q. What qualities unite successful investors?

A. There are lots of successful investors who do things other than what we do. I'm saying this is our philosophy. I think there are several very successful people who kind of take this view, who have been around a long time. People in Sequoia are wonderful and have a very simple direct approach. John Templeton is still great; he still has very long-term views on how to buy stocks.

So we are active in situations to create cheap securities because we have the energy and the knowledge to know how to do the work, to figure out a bankruptcy, to create a cheap stock. But at the end of the day, we want the cheap stock; we're not trading in the bankruptcy just to trade. A lot of Wall Street, and a lot of the activities up front, is just to trade. We don't do that; our turnover rates are low, our fees are lower than most. We just want to perform well for our shareholders.

Q. Do you do a lot of in-house research?

A. We do all in-house research. We give orders to brokers, and we see their research and see what they're saying. But we do most of our own research. I have a dozen analysts who are terrific and we do all our own work.

Q. How important is good research?

A. It's all-important.

Q. Do you market-time at all? Would you go more into cash if you saw no opportunities?

A. That's how it works. Cash balance goes up if we don't find stocks. If we find stocks, cash comes down. We don't come in saying, "Let's raise cash." We come in saying, "Let's buy stocks."

Q. Is the hardest part deciding when to sell?

A. That's really hard because you never know what the buyers are thinking or know or how high something may go. What we kind of do is start selling things when they are about 85% of what we think the company's value is, and we start selling it slowly each day, and if it goes higher, great, we get out of it and we don't look back.

Q. Do you have stop-loss orders?

A. No, but I sit at a trading desk and watch the market all day, so we're very set up to pay attention to the stock market. You know, if you're a doctor and you must be in surgery and the stock goes down, you don't want a big loss, so you'll have a stop order. But you can't be looking at Quotron machines when you're doing brain surgery, right? I sit here all day watching the market, so we don't need stop orders.

Q. What advice do you have for investors?

A. The most important thing, even though most people won't do it, is to read the prospectus. People are lazy. They work really hard to save the money that they have to invest, then all of a sudden they become very lazy. Most people don't want to take the time to call what is usually an 800 number to get what is more or less a pretty simple document. You read it, paying attention to the fees, the terms. The reason you must read it is that the mutual fund industry has found ways to put in both 12b-1 fees and redemption fees as well as loads on the front end, in ways you may not be aware. You might put money in a fund thinking it's a no-load fund, you see, and you may have missed the little asterisk which shows you it's a redemption fee and after the first four years you redeem, you have a 4% discount. Well, that's terrible. So if you read the prospectus, you'll know it's there.

We don't have any of those; we have no load, no 12b-1—nothing.

Q. Any other advice?

A. Do some of your own research, looking back over what the guy's track record was for 5 and 10 years. Five and 10 years gives you bull markets and bear markets, not just bear markets. A quarter or a one-year performance just isn't long enough. You need to look at a record for a minimum of 3 to 5 years, if not 10. You want to know whether it's been the same guy running it and then, if you want to really go a step further, if you're not lazy and you've read the

CHAPTER 38 Mutual Series' Michael Price

prospectus, and you've read the three- to five-year or ten-year performance—and those are musts, those you've got to do—the next step is to take the time to look at the three, four, or five biggest holdings of the fund. That will give you a sense of what the guy buys. And read a few articles about these companies. And before you buy the fund, ask yourself, Do I want to own those companies? Because in effect you're owning those companies, you're paying a guy a hundred basis points to watch over it, right?

You know, one of the things we do here from time to time when the markets are a certain way is, we'll buy closed-end funds at 25 percent discounts. Well, the first thing you do is look at the four or five biggest holdings in the closed-end funds. I remember doing this back in 1984; there was a closed-end fund in London and it was trading at a 25% discount; they had 30% in cash, and the balance of the portfolio was made up in big liquid U.S. oil and gas companies and Royal Dutch Petroleum. So, in effect, I was buying Royal Dutch petroleum at a 25% discount. You couldn't miss—you could *not* miss, you know?

But likewise if I hadn't looked at the holdings, maybe it wouldn't have been Royal Dutch, which is the cheapest and best company in the world. Maybe it would have been some phony Canadian exploration company that trades on the Vancouver Stock Exchange at $13 when it's only worth $2. That's why you have to look at what the fund owns.

That's plenty of work for an individual not in the business to do, but then you'll have some sense of whether you should own a fund.

Q. What lessons have you learned?

A. Well, we make lots of mistakes. I mean, the lesson I learned is this is the way to invest, the value approach. You have to do your own homework. We learned to be diversified; we own a couple of hundred different things. It's very important from time to time to have plenty of cash; you don't have to be invested all the time. Being good all the time is better than being great one year every now and then.

Q. How many funds should someone own?

A. More than one—so you get a feeling for the one you might own, to compare, to pay attention.

Q. What general advice would you give investors?

A. The other thing is at a time like this, when short-term interest rates are very low and a lot of people just don't want 3% on Treasuries, they'll buy something for the hell of it. I think that's real stupid. I think you should take your 3% and keep waiting or looking. Don't be impatient. Wait for the values to show up.

CHAPTER 39

Vanguard/Wellesley Income's Jack Ryan: "Most Income Investors Would Be Better Off Skipping the Highest-Yielding Stocks."

Jack Ryan was born in York, Pennsylvania, in 1949. He obtained a B.S. in Economics from Lehigh University and an M.B.A. from the University of Virginia. He worked for seven years in the manufacturing sector. A Chartered Financial Analyst, he joined the Wellington Management Company in 1981.

Q. Would you describe your strategy?
A. The objective is income. That's the first priority. Growth and appreciation are second. Then I try and buy what I call decent companies, with reasonable valuations. I estimate a reasonable growth rate for a company, and I add that to the dividend yield, then I look at what I have to pay for that—the price-earnings ratio, or price to book.

What you've got in young stocks is growth. And I look at what I have to pay for that. And that's why I say that I try to buy decent companies with reasonable valuations because, unfortunately, the market tends to overpay for growth, number one, and what you're really buying is growth and yield, and you're paying something for it.

So it's obvious that Wal-Mart's a better company than average, but when you buy the stock, you have to say, how much do you have to pay for it? And to the extent I'm right that the market overpays for growth, I think you have to remember that a company can do quite well and the stock doesn't because all the good expectations are already there. And it works on the other side when companies pick up and go through problems. If you are convinced that the long-term growth is still in place, and you have a pretty good yield, and you have decent valuation, here's a chance to buy it, then you don't want to sell it. It's a temporary problem.

I always try and focus on what a reasonable expectation for long-term growth is for this company, like what they do, their proprietary positions, what type of return they can get on a long-term basis, what the growth is—I add that to the yield. I try to maximize that and pay as little as I can.

For every company I own, I have a projected growth rate. That's a judgment call. And for every company I have a yield. I add those two things together, and I use the price-earnings ratio as a marker for what I'm paying in most cases. And I'm aware of that relationship, whenever I look at a new company that I might want to buy: What am I getting and how much am I paying for it? So buying stocks is no different from buying consumer goods.

There are different characteristics of all your investments, and you want to analyze those and try and get a sense of whether those characteristics make the company better or worse than average, then look at what you're paying for it versus what you'd have to pay for an average stock, and see if it makes sense or not. Because it's clear that a well-recognized, above-average company is going to be selling for a well-above-average p-e. But if they're offering you enough, then it's worth paying; if they're not, you go on to something else.

I think the mistake in this business is, people tend to think of a company and the stock as being the same thing, and they're not. And I think you've seen it in cellular telephones and biotechnology. Clearly, those companies have well above-average growth prospects, but how much are you paying for it? Because you're not going to benefit unless the stock does well. If the company does well and the stock doesn't do well, you've lost out as an investor.

Q. And that's why investors look to you.

A. Well, I would recommend to anyone who's interested in investing to try and develop a sense of what things cost. So that when

CHAPTER 39   Vanguard/Wellesley Income's Jack Ryan

they're looking at it, either an above-average growth situation, a below-average growth situation, or strictly a yield situation with no growth, you have to have a sense of what the current market prices are for what you're buying. And this applies to whether it's investing or shopping. You just have to have a sense of what things cost, what you should expect to pay for them. And when you come across a piece of merchandise that you're interested in, you want to see if it's reasonable, because you're not going to get a good return if you're going to start off paying too much for something.

As an investor, you're looking for the future cash flow, which is made up of your dividends plus what you're going to get for the stock when you go to sell it. So you try and maximize the growth and the yield, and you try and minimize how much you're going to pay. And this, to me, is the essence of investing.

It's very simple. The key, too, is you have to stick with your strategy. Because I think you can be a very successful income-oriented investor, or a very successful growth investor, or a very successful manufacturing company investor, whatever. If you figure out what it takes, what makes those stocks tick, and what makes those companies tick, understand it, and then stick with it.

The key is that I've decided to be an income investor. I look at the income first.

Q. What do you think that you've done differently, to explain your unusual success?

A. I stick to my strategy. If it's income, I try and focus on the stocks with above-average dividend yields to begin with, so a stock must have a dividend yield at least equal to the market, and then—very importantly—I try to estimate a reasonable growth rate that I can expect it to yield, and I try and minimize what I pay for it. Now, I stick to that strategy, because you find stocks that have super-high yields and no growth, and in many cases you might as well buy the bonds instead of the stock. If there's no growth, and all you're getting is the yield, you've got a problem—unless it compensates you for the risk you're taking.

Q. You have to know your risk?

A. That's it. I think you do have some risk, especially with the highest-yielding stocks. I think for most income investors, by the way, that they would be better off in the long run skipping the highest-yielding stocks.

Q. Why is that?

A. Because, first of all, many of those high-yielding stocks cut their dividends, and you suffer a capital loss, and problems will crop up where you're forced to sell after that capital loss. The second thing is, in many cases, they have very high yields but no growth, so five years down the road another company—where you gave up point of yield but you've gotten some five years of growth—would actually give you a higher income than you would have had otherwise. So the growth is very important. You want to make sure there's some growth that goes along with that income.

Q. Do you think that successful investors share certain personality characteristics?

A. Yeah, I think some people try and buy an income-oriented stock and then pray that the dividend doesn't go down, whereas I think the thing to do is to buy an income-oriented stock where you're highly confident that the dividend is going to be increased. That's also a checkpoint, by the way, that I do whenever I buy a stock. I look at it and I say, OK, you know the yield is a fact, so I say to myself, "Is there a reasonable expectation for this company to increase its dividend in the next 12 months?" I think an income investor should do this, because if the answer's no, you'd better go back and reexamine why you're buying the stock in the first place. Because if it's a decent company, with a decent valuation, and you can say that they're going to improve their dividend within the next 12 months, you probably have a decent situation to start with. But if your answer is no, they're not going to improve the dividends, then you want to go back to, Why am I buying this? Are there problems that may completely highjack my investment?"

You know, there are thousands of companies out there to invest in, so when you're going into it, you should be pretty confident that you are going to participate as an investor in the progress that company makes. If you can't see progress, then you're just playing the valuation game. And when you buy it, someone else is selling it. Or when you're selling it, someone else is buying it.

And, by the way, this fund has a low-expense shield. I think one of the reasons the fund is successful is the expense shield is low. And I tend to make my purchase and sale decisions against the grain of the market, because what I have found is that what's very popular at the time probably has little appreciation left, and what is unpopu-

CHAPTER 39 Vanguard/Wellesley Income's Jack Ryan

lar at the time oftentimes is the ripest area to do prospecting. I like to look at stocks that are off their highs a little bit.

Q. Do you depend a lot on research?

A. I use a multiplicity of resources. I do a lot of general reading on my own, kind of paying attention to what's happening out there, so that when opportunities are presented to me, I already have knowledge. If somebody's presenting the idea to me, I'd like to think I'm prepared to have something to think about instead of just being a one-way receiver of information.

Q. How important do you think that research is?

A. I think people have to basically do their own research, or hire someone else to do it for them, because remember, the research that your broker sends to you is very marketing-oriented. I think research, although they deny it, is in many cases driven by investment banking relationships. Someone has to pay for the research, and quite often it's corporate finance people who have been trying to get on good terms with companies so they can do deals. I think you have to recognize there is a bias in the research, but there's also a human bias in this that I have found over time, in that the people who are producing the research really don't like to dwell on their mistakes. They like to dwell on things that have done well, so they don't look like idiots . . . and so they like to pull out research reports that they've written on the stocks that have gone up, not on the stocks that have gone down. And I think there's a tendency to focus on successes, not on the stocks that are going down. Again, my example of Bristol Myers is, you can pick up an advantage if you're focusing on stocks that have come down from their high and maybe this is a good entry point.

Q. Do you market-time?

A. No. I don't believe in market timing. You know, there are certain things you can't control, that are unknowable, and one thing is where the market is going. I mean, you can take a guess at it—I take guesses at it all the time, every day—but it's really not a knowable thing. So what I try and focus on is what's knowable. You can look at an investment prospect, you can compare it to what you already own. You know, the characteristics—is it better than what I own already? If it is better than what you already own in your portfolio, why not sell something that's least desirable in your portfolio, add something that's better? If you do that, by definition, at the end of the transaction your portfolio's in a better position.

So I spend the bulk of my time not focusing on whether the market is too high or too low or where it's going. I spend the bulk of my time trying to understand the companies that are out there and available, understanding what I currently own, and finding ways to improve what I own. It's much easier to compare Company A to Company B and say which is the better company now, at this particular point in time, than it is to say I think the stock market's high or low. Most of the popular commentary, whether it's TV shows or periodicals, deals with the market levels. They don't deal with comparing one company versus another. But I think that's something that an average investor will do. So I try and spend my time where I think I can make progress instead of spending my time on something that no one's ever been able to have a successful track record on.

Q. Is it true that the hardest part of investing is knowing when to sell?

A. I think it is. By the way, one of the parts of my strategy is, whenever I buy a security, I have a target sell price for it. When I buy a security, I write down why I bought it, what the different characteristics were, and what drew me to it in the first place. So what I do, when I go into a stock, I kind of know what my target price is for it, so when it gets there, if nothing else has changed, I sell it.

Q. Just like that?

A. Just like that. Because nothing else has changed. When I bought it I said, it's $40 today, I think it's worth $55, so if I'm lucky and my work pays off, and it hits $55, and the market hasn't changed its level, then I sell it, because it's done everything I expected of it. I don't say, well, gee, it's $55, now I think it's worth $70. I don't say that unless there's a reason to take my target price from $55 to $70.

Now here's what happens. We're dealing with the future, and things happen in ways that are unexpected. So, what I like to do is, periodically, when a stock goes up and nothing else has changed, I say if it hits my target price, it's out.

Now the problem is when stocks go down. So I review my investment case for it. What was I thinking at the time I bought it? What's changed in that investment case? If nothing's changed and I still have confidence and the stock's down, then I buy more.

Then you have another problem, which is, the stock's gone down, and quite often when that happens, the investment fundamentals are rerouted. Then the investor is faced with: The stock really isn't hitting my expectations for at least three or four reasons. Of the 10 reasons I bought it for, only one's left, and the stock's down; do I want to continue to own something that really isn't hitting? That's a difficult call.

I am a value-oriented investor, you know, and such investors sometimes buy something at $20, it gets down to $15, and they say, well, I thought it was worth $30, but now I think it's worth $20, so I still have appreciation potential for the new price, which is $15 to $20. So I still think it's worth holding.

Well, you can rationalize that all the way down to zero. You really have to make sure that the reasons that you wanted to own the stock in the first place are still in place. If they're not still in place, then you probably should be leaning toward selling unless you can find real good reasons to own it. Or put another way, if you did not own it today, would you want to buy it? And if you cannot say to yourself, "If I didn't own it today, I would buy it," then you probably should not own it. And you have to be honest with yourself.

This is role-playing, and I try and do it, because you have to recognize that, in a market, every time I buy and sell a stock, there's someone else who's selling and buying it. There's someone else who's taking the exact same information available in the public domain and has reached the opposite conclusion from you. I think it's important to try and say, you know, why is someone ready, willing, and able to be in the market, to make this transaction for me? And you want to go through both sides of your investment case. This is the difference from shopping, where there are goods on the shelf. Someone has taken the same information and reached an opposite conclusion from you, and that should give you pause to think about your investment case.

Q. What lessons have you learned on your own about investing?

A. I've learned to accept the mistakes, that many of them are unavoidable. When you're in this business, you're going to make mistakes all the time. And instead of getting catatonic about it and not taking action, you have to realize that all you can do is try and avoid the avoidable mistakes, and when information unfolds that's totally unexpected, you just reevaluate, try and look at the new investment case. I guess the thing I've learned is you really should expect the unexpected, and when it happens, you try and objectively look at it, and not worry about what you paid for something, or why you paid for it. Try and deal with the new information and incorporate it in your investment case.

The other thing I've found increasingly is that management does matter. And it's real hard to judge management. If you own something or if you want to own something, you should try and understand the quality of that management because increasingly I have found that they make a difference; there's a reason why they get paid these big salaries, some of which are deserved, but there's a reason why they're paid that, and they can make millions and millions and millions of dollars of difference to the progress of the firm. So I have found that I do try and spend more time in understanding what the management strategy is, what they're trying to do, if they're effective, if they're decisive, if they've adjusted to a changing environment, if strategically what they're trying to do still makes sense within the competitive arena. It's hard to do that, but you have to make a cut at it, because there might be a mosaic that develops that you can learn from.

And I think the key is to stay invested in companies that will continue to participate in the upward progress of the economy, that will continue to turn out profits, and will just participate in the economy. And that's the key, to construct a portfolio that's going to continue to participate in the upswing.

If something is obvious, it's probably the wrong thing to do.

There is a little bit of pain in investing if you want to make money. If you keep doing what feels comfortable, well, you're just late. You have to take a certain amount of discomfort when you take investment action, and that's the only way you're going to make money. If you're always going for comfort, you're going to get negative returns. And the only place you can find comfort is in money-market type securities, where they're paying you a low rate of return.

There's a reason why stocks and bonds have to pay more than money markets, so by definition, you have to take risks if you want to make money. If you feel like you're not taking any risk on an investment, you're probably taking incredible risks.

CHAPTER 39 Vanguard/Wellesley Income's Jack Ryan

Q. How many different funds do you think a person should own?

A. I think a person should probably have no more than 10 to 15 funds or stocks, that is to say the universe should be no larger than their ability to monitor what they own. I think somewhere in the 10 to 15 range you can get the diversification that removes a certain degree of unanticipated risk.

Q. Are there any investors you admire greatly?

A. I don't know other investors that well. I try and pay attention to companies instead of to other investors. I would say that what someone should do is they should look for a reputable organization, look for funds with a good long-term track record but a short-term underperforming record. If they're still the same manager and they're still doing what they said they'd be doing, and they've underperformed recently, that's exactly when you want to buy. You see you want to kind of funnel your money toward the things that have recently underperformed but they still have good long-term records. You want to look for low fees. Never buy what is sold to you; something that has to be sold to you probably has some undesirable characteristics—unless you really trust the person putting it in front of you and know them quite well.

Q. What books would you recommend?

A. I think people are much better off if they read annual reports instead of investment books because if you don't know what you're investing in, you can't apply what you've learned. I would also recommend that you read broadly, because first of all, you'll be a more interesting person and you'll have more fun; and secondly, what you really want to do is improve your judgment, and you want to be able to recognize change, discontinuity, before someone else does, and that's how you get to the areas where the capital returns are improving.

CHAPTER 40

Fidelity Equity-Income II's Brian Posner: "I Try to Avoid Cheap Stocks That *Should* Be Cheap."

Brian S. Posner received a B.A. in History from Northwestern in 1983 and an M.B.A. from the University of Chicago in 1987. That year he joined Fidelity as an oil and insurance analyst. He has also managed Fidelity Value Fund, Fidelity Select Life Insurance, Fidelity Select Property-Casualty Portfolio, and Fidelity Select Energy Portfolio.

Q. Could you describe your fund?

A. As an equity-income fund, my fund is probably in the spectrum of risk a relatively conservative fund. However, the fund is structured by prospectus in such a way that it is clearly not the most conservative of equity funds—it's not a utility fund or a balanced fund or one of the more traditional equity-income funds. We're probably closer to the growth-and-income category. What I'm trying to do is, while limiting the risk as much as possible, look for situations that can present upside potential. The way I do that is by putting together a portfolio where, when I look at the valuations in aggregate, I have relatively low price to earnings. However, the earnings growth potential and the expected future growth rate should exceed that of the general market.

I'm looking at a number of special situations: A lot of medium-cap companies that may be undiscovered by Wall Street; restructurings; cyclicals that have been depressed for various reasons. In general, what I want to find are growth stocks that people don't recognize are growth stocks, and that as a result aren't valued like growth stocks, where you get the most upside leverage—not just earning growth, but also where valuations are low. That's what happens with growth stocks. If I can find a company that's trading at a relatively modest multiple, yet has a history of growth that's unrecognized, then it can be a very exciting story.

What I try to avoid, the most difficult component of this strategy, is "wasting assets," cheap stocks that should be cheap. It's easy to seduced by a low p-e. However, many times there are many good reasons why a stock has a low p-e. What I have to do is, on the one hand look at the opportunity, and on the other hand make sure that what I'm buying is not a wasting asset, where whatever value I ascribe to the company is not going to diminish over time.

Q. Why are you in particular successful?

A. A lot of others have been doing it much longer. I feel like a baseball player who's had a few good years. And the older players and the retired players say, let's see in 15 years whether he's really a Hall of Famer. I'm really uncomfortable answering that. If you ask me in 15 years, and I have the same sort of record, I would feel more comfortable. As good as the results have been over the last couple of years, I'm not at the point of thinking that I'm a genius. I've been fortunate—my timing has been pretty darn good. Given the sort of stocks I like, 1991 was a difficult year, it was really a growth market. But given my approach, I was able to keep up. Traditional value investors failed in that market because of a focus exclusively on traditional value-type stocks, whereas I spent a lot of time on companies that were considered restructurings or special situations, like banks.

1992 was also a relatively nice environment for value investors versus growth investors, and in this environment I *should* be propelled forward beyond the results of the growth investor, and I have been.

Q. What distinguishes successful investors from others?

A. A combination of two inherently contradictory traits: Discipline and flexibility. On the one hand, there are people who are almost pure traders. The way I look at a company is, I take investing very seriously. I try to value a company by imagining I can buy 100 percent of the company at the current stock price. What kind of return might I get? That sort of ignores issues like momentum and all that.

On the other hand, for the last few years or so there have been certain groups that did very well. I own very little health care. There will be a point, I believe, when I should own health care and that's where the flexibility comes in. The fact that I have this affinity for investing in financials doesn't necessarily mean it will make sense in three years. A successful investor will know when the financials have been played out, when the fundamentals are deteriorating or the equities are fully valued and have to look in other areas.

So that's why I don't ignore those companies today; I'm constantly calling them and visiting them. But in terms of how I value them, I don't think they're ready today but someday they will be ready. Given my approach, I can never say no, I will never own X industry or X company.

Q. Do successful investors share any personality characteristics, like patience?

A. I don't know. I'm a relatively patient investor and think certain people are more patient than others. I think so much of it is emotional—you have to have a real understanding of how the numbers play out, but in the end it's emotional. Understanding that things go up and go down, and whether a stock goes up or down in the short term doesn't necessarily mean you're right or wrong. And you have to live with that. And that's difficult to do, especially for a beginner.

If one day you found something, and on day two it's down 5%, and nothing's happened, you can't let that get to you; if you can, you buy more. That's a tough thing to do.

Q. Do you depend on a lot of in-house research?

A. Almost exclusively. I have a number of outside contacts who are helpful, but one of the advantages of working at a place like Fidelity is the in-house resources. All the fund managers were analysts, we all speak the same language. That raises the issue, if you take that fish out of the water, how good is that fish going to be? I cannot separate my success from what Fidelity has provided me, in terms of human capital and hard resources, so I'm not an island unto myself. If I were somewhere else, maybe my results would be different—better or worse.

Q. Do you market-time?

A. No, I don't think anyone has ever done it successfully.

I used to be a trader, very frustrating and difficult. Market-timing never seems to work. Another reason is: If there were perfect liquidity I could do it, but on any day a stock may not be available for me to buy, or the market may not be there for me to sell. I have to sort of look through events and be able to look at things that are disturbing other people when I'm buying a stock. Frequently, if I'm looking at a situation that's a turnaround or a restructuring, the sort of companies that have cyclical pressures, rather than wait for that point in time when the earnings start going up, I have to be there when things start to stabilize. Frequently that does mark the bottom and is the right time to buy anyway. But I can't wait for the rest of the world to realize what's going on. My position is too large.

Q. Would you go more into cash?

A. I could increase or decrease the aggressiveness of the portfolio, but I'm hesitant to do that. Market moves on the upside occur during very short periods of time. If you remove just the four best quarters over the 20 years that ended on June 30, 1992, the compounded annual return on stocks drops from 11% to 8%. I think it makes more sense to remain fully invested.

Q. Is deciding when to sell the hardest decision?

A. It is difficult, but I don't get caught up in momentum, so that sort of pressure isn't there. I ask myself, if I were to take out 100 percent of the company at the current stock price, what kind of return would I get? If the expected return is less than what I can get in other vehicles, especially in cash, then I sell. Or the fundamentals are deteriorating. My approach is to be relatively early in buying stocks, so that maybe I catch the very beginnings of moves, and I try to leave earlier than others.

As this fund has become quite large, I want excitement to be generated. So if valuations become frothy, that's good.

Q. What advice would you give investors?

A. You have to do lots of research. The more time I spend doing this job, the more I realize how difficult it is. You should also have as much understanding as possible of what the fund manager is trying to do. Just buying the hot funds can really be dangerous. As

CHAPTER 40 Fidelity Equity-Income II's Brian Posner

Peter Lynch said, people will spend four times more deciding what washing machine or car to buy than when they plunk down $5,000 to buy a stock or mutual fund.

Q. What lessons have you learned from your mistakes?

A. I've learned from lots of mistakes. One of the things I learned is the importance of financial statements. If you read them, over time, you can develop a real sense of what a company is trying to do—or is not doing. And many times, some of my larger disasters were the result of not listening to what the financial statements were telling me.

I've also learned that you don't worry about halves and quarters. I've stopped looking for substantial returns from each of my investments. If something goes up or down in the short run, it doesn't mean you're wrong. It's something you always should remember.

CHAPTER 41

Oakmark's Robert J. Sanborn: "All in All, You Need Just Three Stock Funds."

Born in Boston, Robert Sanborn, 35, received a B.A. from Dartmouth in 1980 and an M.B.A. from the University of Chicago in 1983. In 1986 he earned a Certified Financial Analyst designation. He joined Harris Associates (which formerly was the adviser to Ralph Wanger's Acorn Fund) as a portfolio manager in 1988. From 1983 to 1987 he worked for the State Teachers Retirement System of Ohio.

Q. What explains your sensational 1992 performance?

A. There are three main reasons: (1) the largest part of our portfolio was in Liberty Media, which did unbelievably—up threefold. It's a big cable company; (2) twenty percent of the fund was in the financial/insurance area, which has done well; and (3) we had no big losers—nothing over 10%. The core of our style is not to lose much on the downside and to do well on the upside.

Q. Do you have any other funds?

A. Oakmark International, which is run with the same value-oriented philosophy. But we're primarily an investment firm, not a marketing firm, so we're not going to have a lot of funds.

Q. Are you planning to close the fund if it gets too large?

A. We're managing $2 billion now, through our private accounts, and we're still finding good stocks, so we don't plan to close. We started last year with $4 million and now we have $200 million.

Q. How many funds should someone own, besides Oakmark?

A. I talk to our shareholders, and my impression is that They own too many funds—9, 10, 11 equity funds. And because they overdiversify, they obtain only average results. In my own case, I have a long-term time frame, so I'm 80% in Oakmark and 20% in Oakmark International. If I were my dad, who's 65, I'd put half my money into a low-expense fixed-income fund, like one of Vanguard's, 40% in Oakmark, and 10% in Oakmark International.

All in all, I think you need just three stock funds: one international and two domestic. One of the domestic might be value-oriented, like Oakmark, and the other might be growth-oriented, like Monetta, which is also in Chicago.

Q. What is your strategy?

A. We have five guidelines.

We have a long-term point of view, and we try to buy stocks at prices that are less than their value. We believe that price and value will converge over time.

We like a shareholder-oriented management.

We try to be independent thinkers.

We trade infrequently—so as to minimize taxes.

And we don't overdiversify. We have 40 holdings, and the top 20 constitute 65% of the portfolio.

APPENDIX

For More Information . . .

For mutual-fund literature:

Investment Company Institute
1600 M Street, N.W.
Washington, DC 20036
202-293-7700

Mutual Fund Educational Alliance
1900 Erie Street, Suite 120
Kansas City, MO 64116

100% No-Load Council
1501 Broadway, Suite 312
NY, NY 10036

For mutual-fund newsletters:

These newsletters are associated with some of the authorities listed in Chapter 4. You can write or phone any newsletter for a free copy.

**NoLoad Fund*X
215 Montgomery Street
San Francisco, CA 94104
415-986-7979
$100 per year

Donoghue's Moneyletter
PO Box 6640
Holliston, MA 01746
508-429-5930
$49 for three months; $87 per year

No-Load Fund Investor
PO Box 318
Irvington-on-Hudson, NY 10533
914-693-7420
$119 per year

L/G No-Load Fund Analyst
4 Orinda Way, Suite 230-D
Orinda, CA 94563
1-800-776-9555
$169 per year

Fund Exchange
1200 Westlake Avenue North
Suite 507
Seattle, WA 98109-3530
1-800-423-4893
$49 for six months, $99 per year

Morningstar Mutual Funds
53 West Jackson Blvd., Suite 460
Chicago, IL 60604
$395 per year

Mutual Fund Investing
7811 Montrose Road
Potomac, MD 20854
1-800-722-9000
$99 per year

**The Outlook
(Standard & Poor's)**
25 Broadway
New York, NY 10004
212-208-8786
$268 per year

Value Line Mututal Fund Survey
220 East 42nd Street
New York, NY 10017-5891
$295 per year

Other Books by the Author

Keys to Investing in Mutual Funds, second edition
Barron's Educational Series
250 Wireless Boulevard
Hauppauge, NY 11788
1-800-645-3476 (in New York, 1-800-257-5729)
1992, $4.95

Mutual Fund Timing & Switching Strategies
Irwin Professional Publishing
1333 Burr Ridge Parkway
Burr Ridge, IL 60521
1-800-634-3966
1991, $19.95

The Ultimate Stock Picker's Guide
Irwin Professional Publishing
1333 Burr Ridge Parkway
Burr Ridge, IL 60521
1-800-634-3966

GLOSSARY

Aggressive Growth Fund A fund that seeks maximum capital gains. It usually remains fully invested in stocks at all times; it buys small, speculative companies and depressed stocks; and it may employ techniques like selling short and using leverage. Aggressive growth funds tend to be especially volatile.

All-Weather Fund A fund that does well in bull and bear markets.

Alternative Minimum Tax: A special tax that certain people must pay for taking advantage of too many tax breaks.

Appreciation Growth in value of an asset.

Asset Allocation Fund A fund that either keeps a fixed percentage of its assets in various instruments—bonds, stocks, precious-metals stocks, real-estate stocks—or varies the percentages, depending on where the fund managers think the investment markets are heading. A true asset-allocation fund has some investments in inflation-resistant hard assets (precious metals, real estate).

Bear Market Time when stocks (or other investments) keep sinking in value, despite occasional rallies, or when stocks remain at depressed levels.

Balanced Fund A fund that invests in both stocks and bonds—typically 60% in stocks, 40% in bonds.

Barbell: A way of investing in fixed-income securities, so that short maturities are balanced by longer-term maturities.

Basic Value Investing Investment strategy that concentrates on buying seemingly undervalued stocks, based on their price-earnings ratios, price to book value, and other indicators.

Basis Point In bond yields, 0.01%. If a bond's yield goes from 10% to 11%, it has increased by 100 basis points.

Blue Chip Stock of a large, prosperous, well-established company. The 30 stocks in the Dow Jones Industrial Average—including IBM, AT&T, and Exxon—are unquestionably blue chips.

Bond A debt instrument that pays a regular interest, whether or not the company issuing the bond is making money. Debt instruments are "senior" securities: Their holders must be paid before a company pays owners of its stock.

Bond Fund A fund that invests mainly in corporate, municipal, and U.S. Treasury securities. Such a fund emphasizes income rather than capital gains.

Bond Rating System of grading bonds on their ability to pay their obligations. Standard & Poor's ratings range from AAA (extremely unlikely to default) to D (in default). Moody's ratings are similar.

Bottom Up Method of investing in which the investor concentrates on buying attractive stocks, whatever the broad trends of the market or the economy. See Top Down.

Broker/Dealer A firm, like Merrill Lynch, that buys and sells load mutual funds and other securities to the public.

Bull Market Time when stocks (or other securities) keep climbing in value, despite occasional stumbles. Sometimes the boundary between bull and bear markets isn't sharp.

Bullet A way of investing in fixed-income securities in which the maturities are neither short term nor long term but intermediate term.

Buy and Hold Investment strategy that entails buying shares of stock or a mutual fund for the long term and selling them only in special circumstances, such as after a long-term loss. See Market Timing.

Cash Equivalents Short-term obligations, like Treasury bills.

Closed Fund A fund that has stopped issuing new shares. Funds close either because they are so large that the managers cannot find enough good investments, or because the manager prefers investing only in small companies and cannot cope with large amounts of money.

Certificate of Deposit Conservative debt instruments provided by a bank or savings and loan, with maturities varying from months to several years. Usually there are penalties if an investor cashes in a CD before maturity. With a floating rate CD, the interest rate changes in line with the prime rate.

Closed-end Investment Company A mutual fund whose shares are bought and sold on an exchange or over-the-counter, by investors trading among themselves. A closed-end fund issues only a limited number of shares. See Open-end Investment Company.

Collateralized Mortgage Obligation A complicated mortgage-backed security.

Common Stock Security representing ownership of a public corporation's assets.

Contrarian Investing Buying securities cheaply when other investors are pessimistic; selling securities dearly (at a high price) when other investors are optimistic.

Corporate Bond Fund A fund that invests in corporate bonds, which may be high rated or low rated, and have short-term, medium-term, or long-term maturities.

Current Yield Dividends paid to investors, as a percentage of the current price.

Distributions Payments that a mutual fund makes to its shareholders, from the sales of its securities, from interest, from dividends—or a return of the shareholder's original investment.

Diversification Spreading investments over a variety of different securities in order to reduce risk.

Diversified Investment Company Company whose investments are limited to no more than 5% in a single issue, and no more than 10% of that issuer's outstanding securities; at least 75% of its assets must be in varied securities.

Dividends: Money (or stock) that a company pays the owners of its stock, usually four times a year.

Dollar-Cost Averaging Investing the same amount of money at regular intervals so that when securities are low-priced, you buy more shares. A method of diversifying the prices at which you buy securities.

Dow Jones Industrial Average Model for the stock market as a whole. It consists of 30 blue-chip stocks.

DRIP: A dividend reinvestment program that certain companies offer to owners of their stocks.

GLOSSARY

Estate Tax A tax assessed on transfers of assets after your death. Generally, transfers that do not exceed $600,000, and transfers to your surviving spouse, are not taxable.

Equities: Stocks, real estate, and other assets that an investor owns, as opposed to bonds, where an investor lends money.

Equity-Income A type of mutual fund that concentrates on high-paying common stocks.

Equity REIT A real estate investment trust that concentrates on buying shares of real estate companies. See Mortgage REIT.

Event Risk The danger that a bond will lose value because of special situations, such as the issuer being subjected to a leveraged buyout and acquiring a great deal of new debt.

Fair-Weather Fund A fund that excels in bull markets but gives a mediocre or poor performance in bear markets. See Foul-Weather Fund.

Family Group of mutual funds under one umbrella, typically consisting of a stock, a bond fund, and a money-market fund.

Family Partnership An arrangement to own real estate or businesses so that you can transfer portions of the assets to your children's educational funds, without losing control over your assets.

Fixed-Income Fund A fund that invests mainly in bonds and preferred stock.

Flexible See Asset Allocation.

Formula Investing Investing according to mechanical techniques, such as dollar-cost averaging.

Foul-Weather Fund A fund that excels in bear markets, one explanation being that the fund invests in securities that are already undervalued. See Fair-Weather Fund.

Front-End Load Sales commission investors pay at the time they buy shares of a mutual fund.

General Obligation Bonds Bonds that pay holders from their basic taxing authority—as opposed to revenue bonds.

Gift Tax A tax you may have to pay when you give away large assets. Generally, gifts of under $10,000—or tuition paid directly to the school—are not taxable.

Global Fund One that invests in foreign as well as domestic stocks.

GNMA Fund A fund that invests in mortgage securities issued by the Government National Mortgage Association.

Government Bond Fund A fund that invests mostly in Treasuries, but also possibly in government agency bonds and mortgage-backed securities.

Growth Fund A fund that invests in companies that seem to have bright futures in view of their growth rates.

Growth and Income Fund A fund that invests in growth stocks as well as high-income, blue-chip stocks.

Hedge Fund A fund that not only invests in securities but may also sell short or write options in order to protect itself from losses.

Income Fund A fund that stresses current income rather than growth of capital. Such funds may be mainly invested in high-yielding stocks and in bonds, but mainly in bonds.

Index: Model of an investment market—stocks, bonds, utilities, health-care stocks, and so forth.

Index Fund A fund that attempts to emulate the performance of an index, like the Standard & Poor's 500 or the Shearson-Lehman Bond Index.

International Fund A fund that invests in the securities of foreign corporations or governments.

Investment Objective Goals of a mutual fund, such as long-term capital gains, with income secondary.

Investment Grade Bond Bonds rated BBB, Standard & Poor's fourth-highest category, and above.

Junk Bonds Bonds rated BB or below by Standard & Poor's. Such bonds are not as safe as investment grade bonds, but they pay higher interest. Also called "high yield bonds."

Kiddie Tax: Income of children under age 14 can be taxed at their parents' highest tax rate.

Ladder Arranging the maturities of one's fixed-income investments so they become due at different times, such as one year, two years, and three years.

Limited Partnership Investment group made up of a general partner, who manages a project, and the limited partners, who invest money and whose liability is limited.

Liquidity Measure of how readily an asset can be sold for cash. If an asset can readily be sold, but at a loss, its liquidity is compromised. In this respect, a money-market fund is far more liquid than a stock fund.

Load Commission charge that buyers of certain mutual funds must pay. The load goes to the stockbroker and the distributor, or—in the case of most low-load funds—to the fund itself. Generally, low-load funds charge 1% to 3%; medium loads, 3% to 6%; and full loads, 6% to 8.5%. No-load funds sell their shares directly to investors.

Market Timing Attempting to buy securities near the end of a bear market and to sell them near the end of a bull market—in other words, to buy low and sell high. See Buy and Hold.

Maturity When a loan—or a bond—is due to be paid off by the debtor or by the issuing company.

Money-Market Fund A fund that invests in debt obligations with maturities of no more than a year. To keep the principal unchanging, usually at $1 a share, the fund varies the yield. Banks' funds are called money market deposit accounts.

Mortgage-Backed Securities Shares of a pool of mortgages, issued by Fannie Mae (Federal National Mortgage Association), Freddie Mac (Federal Home Loan Mortgage Corporation), or Ginnie Mae (Government National Mortgage Association). Investors receive regular payments of principal and interest from the underlying mortgages.

Mortgage REIT Real estate investment trust that concentrates on lending money to builders and buyers. See Equity REIT.

Municipal Bond Fund A fund that invests in tax-exempt bonds issued by states, cities, and local governments. The bonds may be short-, intermediate-, or long-term, and they may be high-rated or low-rated.

GLOSSARY

Net Assets Value of a fund's holdings, minus debts, such as taxes owed.

Net Asset Value Price per share of a fund: net assets divided by number of shares outstanding.

No-Load A fund that does not charge a front-end commission. A "pure" no-load also has no deferred sales charge, no redemption fee, and no 12b-1 fee.

Open-End Investment Company A fund that can continually issue more shares and thus add to its net assets. Such a fund also buys shares directly from its customers and sells shares directly to its customers. See Closed-End Investment Company.

Over-the-Counter Market in which securities are bought and sold through dealers, not on the floor of an exchange. OTC stocks are typically those of smaller companies.

Performance How well a fund has fared over a certain time period, usually measured by capital gains, dividends, and interest the fund has earned.

Portfolio Various securities held by an individual or a fund.

Portfolio Manager Person or committee that makes buy-and-sell decisions for a fund.

Premium Percentage that a security's price exceeds its net asset value per share. A bond paying high interest may trade at a premium.

Price-Earnings Ratio Price per share of a stock, divided by its last 12 months of earnings (or estimated earnings for the next year). The p/e ratio indicates how popular a stock is by reflecting how much investors are willing to pay for its earning power.

Prime Rate The interest rate that lenders charge their best customers.

Prospectus: Official document describing a mutual fund. It must be furnished to investors.

Real Estate Investment Trust Company that buys real estate, lends money to real estate companies, or both. Usually a REIT's shares are publicly traded.

Redemption Fee Charge a fund may levy, especially if an investor sells shares purchased recently.

Revenue Bonds Bonds that pay their holders from money the issuer earns—as from a turnpike authority.

Risk Either the volatility of an instrument, or the possibility that the investment will lose value.

Risk Tolerance: Ability of a person to accept what may be temporary losses from an investment.

Sales Charge Commission an investor must pay to buy shares of certain load mutual funds or of a limited partnership.

Sector Stocks in one industry.

Secular Long-term.

Securities Stocks, bonds, options, warrants, or other instruments that signify a corporation's obligations to an investor.

Securities and Exchange Commission (SEC) Federal agency, created in 1934, that administers the securities laws.

Sell Short To borrow a security through a broker, sell it, and buy it back later. Short sellers expect a security's price to decline.

Small Company Fund A fund of small-company stocks—the size usually being measured in terms of capitalization, which is stock price times shares outstanding.

Special Situation Stock that is expected to benefit from a new development, such as an important new product or management change.

Specialty A fund that restricts its horizon to certain stocks: utilities, health care, regional banks, gold, and so forth.

Spendthrift A section of a trust agreement that attempts to limit the rights of creditors or others to reach trust assets.

Spread Difference between the bid and the offer prices on a stock or bond.

Sprinkle Power The authority given to a trustee of a trust for your children to distribute income to the children most in need.

Standard & Poor's 500 Popular microcosm of the stock market, based on the prices of 500 widely held common stocks.

Standard Deviation: Volatility of an investment, measured by comparing its average price with the degree of its ups and downs.

Time Horizon How long you can remain invested before you will need your principal. The longer your time horizon, the greater the chance that you will escape needing your money in a down market.

Top Down Method of investing in which the investor looks at general economic trends, then decides which industries and companies will benefit. See Bottom Up.

Total Return Profit or loss that a mutual fund has achieved over a period of time, including capital gains or losses, interest and dividends, and expenses. It is expressed as a percentage of the original value of the assets.

Treasury Debts of the U.S. Government. The maturities of Treasury bills are up to one year, of notes, 2 to 10 years, and of bonds, 10 to 30 years.

Trust An arrangement to own assets for your children's benefit that can provide for management of the assets, and possibly some protection from creditors.

Turnover Ratio Trading activity of a mutual fund, calculated by dividing the lesser of purchases or sales for the fund's fiscal year by the monthly average of the portfolio's net assets. Excluded are securities that mature within a year. A turnover ratio of 100% is the equivalent of a complete portfolio turnover.

12b-1 Fee Amount that a fund takes from its assets—and thus from its shareholders—to pay for distribution and marketing costs. Usually .25% to 1.25% of assets. Also called a hidden load.

Uniform Gifts/Transfers to Minors Act A custodial arrangement created under state law that can provide you with some control over assets transferred to your minor children.

Unit Investment Trust A fund that buys a portfolio of securities—usually bonds—and normally holds them until maturity.

Volatility Fluctuations in the price of a security or index of securities.

Will A legal document that provides for how your assets are transferred on your death.

Wilshire 5000 Model of all stocks, including those on the New York Stock Exchange, the American Exchange, and over-the-counter. The Wilshire is one of the broadest indexes, and includes over 6,000 stocks.

Yield Regular income from a fund, expressed as a percentage of the fund's average net asset value, not including capital gains or losses.

Yield to Maturity Yield (as above) plus any certain gains or loss on the price of a bond from now until the time it comes due, expressed as a percentage of the bond's price.

Yield Curve Graph comparing the interest rates of similar bonds according to their maturities. Usually long-term rates are higher than short-term rates. When short-term rates are higher, there is a negative yield curve.

Zero Coupon Bond A bond sold at a small fraction of its face value. It gradually appreciates, but no interest is paid to investors, who must nonetheless pay taxes on the interest (except for tax-exempt bonds). Earnings accumulate until maturity.

INDEX

AAII, 8
Abe, Shuhei, 98
Acorn Fund, 61, 62, 102, 107, 109, 257
Addison-Wesley Publishing Company, 24
Aggressive growth stock funds, 16, 17, 31 32, 33–35, 62, 64–67
Aggressive stock funds, 6, 19
Alabama, University of, 213
Alger Small Cap, 62
Alliance Short-Term, 62
American Association of Individual Investors; *See* AAII
American Funds, 108, 109, 115
American Heritage, 90, 102, 112
American Money Report, 26
American University, 24
Apple Computer, 197
Artisan Partners, 67, 102
Artisan Small Cap, 63, 67–68
Askew, Peter B., 57
Asset allocation stock fund, 16, 18, 19
Assets, 20
Astra, 112
Athey, Preston, 36, 195 200
Auriana, Lawrence, 65

Babson Enterprise, 62
Bailard, Biehl & Kaiser, 25
Bailey, Tom, 170, 222
Balanced stock funds, 6, 16, 18, 19, 49 52, 63, 78
Baltimore Gas and Electric, 192
BAMCO, 90
Baron, Ronald, 73, 90
Baron Asset, 89–91
Baron Capital, 73
Baron Growth & Income, 63, 72–73
Barron's, 24, 26
Barrow, Hanley, Mewhinny & Struss, 88
Barrow, James P., 88
Baxter, Chris, 182–183
Bear markets, 129–131
Benham GNMA & Income, 62

Berger, 109
Berger 100, 62
Berry, Burton, 23, 85, 89, 121–122, 125, 131, 148, 149, 151, 154, 158, 168, 173
BJ Group, 25
Blanchard Short-Term Global, 62
Blue Book of Mutual Funds Reports, 26
Boettcher & Company, 219
Bogle, John C., 177–179
Bond funds, classification of, 6
Bond Market Fund, 229–230
Bonnel, Arthur J., 97, 102
Boroson, Warren, 23, 85, 89
Boroson's Mutual Fund Digest, 24
Boston University, 24
Boyd, Christopher K., 35
Brandywine, 30, 62, 64–65, 103
Bray, Catherine H., 80
Brouwer, Kurt, 24, 85, 109, 112, 126, 130, 140, 145, 148, 151, 159, 164, 167
Brouwer & Janachoski, 24
Buffett, Warren, 217, 222
Bull & Bear, 112
Bull markets, 129–131
Business Week, 203
Buy-and-holders, 120–121

Calvert Asset Management, 91
Calvert Strategic Growth, 89, 91
Carret, Phil, 190
Cash Manager, 24
Castegren, Hakan, 102, 159, 206
CDA, 26
CDA/Wiesenberger, 26
CGM Mutual, 63, 78, 90
Charles Schwab Investment Management, 95
Chen/Price Jr., 93
Chicago, University of, 26, 27, 251, 257
Christian Science Monitor, 26
Clipper, 102, 107
Closed-end investment companies, versus open-ends, 123–126

269

Cohen & Steers Realty, 62
Collins, James O., 92
Colonial Newport Tiger, 63, 102
Colonial Newport Tiger T, 74
Colorado, University of, 219
Columbia Special, 62
Columbia University, 26
Complete Money Market Guide (Donoghue), 24
Connecticut Conference of Municipalities, 24
Continental Bank, 233
Core funds, typical, 122
Cornell University, 26
Corporate bond funds, 6, 32
Corporate bond stock funds, 63 64, 79–81
Corporate fixed-income fund, 18, 19
Counsellors Emerging Growth Fund; *See* Warburg Pincus Emerging Growth
Craig, James P., 70, 102, 213–218
Czepiel, Robert C., 15

DAL Investment Co., 23
Danoff, Will, 34
Dartmouth College, 257
Dater, Elizabeth B., 67
Davis, Christopher C., 104
Davis, Shelby, 101 103, 104
Davis New York Venture, 104
Davis Selected Advisers, 104
Dean Witter, 111, 112
Dean Witter Dividend Growth, 107
Denver, University of, 219
DFA, 108
Dodge & Cox, 50, 109, 201–203
Dodge & Cox Balanced, 32, 49–50, 78, 86
Dominion Insight Growth, 89, 92
Donoghue, William E., 24, 86, 89, 109, 120–122, 130, 139, 140, 154, 155, 164, 167, 173
Donoghue's Money Fund Report, 24
Donoghue's MoneyLetter, 24
Dow Jones Industrial Average, 9, 170
Dow Jones Industrials, 199
The Dow Jones Irwin Mutual Fund Yearbook, 24
Drexel University, 181
Dreyfus, 111, 112, 113, 223
Dreyfus Balanced, 63, 78
Droms, William G., 24, 85, 89, 124, 131, 151, 168, 173

Duke University, 206

Eaton Vance, 112
Edgemont Asset Management, 65
Egener, Stanley, 110
Elijah, Ronald E., 101–102, 105
Eli Lilly, 197
EQSF Advisers, 96–97
Equity income stock funds, 6, 16, 18, 19, 31–32, 45–47, 63, 77
Equity style box, 7
ERISA, 218
Eveillard, Jean-Marie, 76, 157
Excellence in Financial Journalism Award, 24
Expense ratio, 19

Federal Home Loan banks, 55
Federal Housing Administration, 55
Federated, 112
Fees, 138
Felske, Derek, 35
Fidelity Asset Manager, 62, 85
Fidelity Balanced, 63, 78, 85
Fidelity Capital and Income, 62
Fidelity Contrafund, 31, 33–34
Fidelity Destiny, 61
Fidelity Disciplined Equity, 62, 102
Fidelity Equity-Income, 29, 32, 63, 77
Fidelity Equity-Income II, 29, 30, 46, 85, 251– 255
Fidelity Europe, 62
Fidelity Fund, 62
Fidelity Growth and Income, 31, 38–39
Fidelity Health Care, 63
Fidelity High-Income Muni, 62
Fidelity Limited Term Muni, 62
Fidelity Low-Priced Stock, 30, 63, 68–69
Fidelity Magellan, 61, 103–104, 143–145, 149
Fidelity Management & Research, 12, 34, 39, 46, 68, 77, 78, 103, 108, 109, 112, 141, 149, 158, 159, 179
Fidelity Puritan, 62, 63, 78
Fidelity Select Energy Portfolio, 251
Fidelity Select Health Care, 77–78
Fidelity Select Life Insurance, 251
Fidelity Select Property-Casualty Portfolio, 251
Fidelity Selects, 122
Fidelity Short-Term Bond, 62

INDEX

Fidelity Utilities Income, 62
Fidelity Value Fund, 251
Financial Planning, 26
Financial Success for Salaried People (Pope), 26
Firestone, Karen, 78
First Investors, 111, 112
Fixed-income funds, 18, 19, 32, 54–59
 corporate bonds, 54–55
 government bonds, 55–57
 international/global bonds, 57
 municipal bonds, 58–59
Flexfunds Muirfield, 86
Fogle, Glenn, 207–210
Forbes, 24
Forbes Honor Roll, 129
Fortune, 203
Founders, 109
Founders Discovery, 62
FPA Paramount, 102, 145
Franklin, 112, 223
Franklin Rising Dividends, 62
Franklin/Templeton, 116
Fred Alger Management, 219
Friess, Foster S., 64, 101–102
Friess Associates, 64
Fund Exchange, 25
Fund performance, understanding, 15–20
Funds
 best families, 107–110
 best load, 115–116
 best overlooked, 89–99
 evaluating, 127–131
 experts, 23–27
 frequently recommended, 31–32
 and individual securities, 167–168
 interviews with top managers, 175, 258
 introduction, 3–9
 managers performance, 157–160
 and market-timers, 169–174
 performance, 153–156
 portfolio assembly, 161–165
 portfolio managers, 101–105
 runners-up, 61–84
 selling, 147–152
 single best, 85–88
 size, 143–145
 thirty-three best, 29–59
 worst families, 111–113
 worst handicaps, 137–141

Fuss, Daniel J., 79, 187–190

Gabelli, Mario, 102, 112, 140, 157, 231
Gabelli Growth, 62
GAM International, 31, 44–45, 102
GAM International Management, 44
Gateway Index Plus, 30, 85
Gateway Index Trust, 90, 102
Georgetown University, 24
George Washington University, 26
Gibson, James, 102
Gipson/Grey, 95
Global bond funds, 6
Government bond funds, 6, 32
Government bond stock funds, 64, 81–82
Government fixed-income fund, 18, 19
Government National Mortgage Association (GNMA), 55, 56
Graham, Ben, 139
Granville, Joe, 230
Gray, Susan E., 84
Green, Frederick W., 86
Gross, William H., 82, 101–102, 205–206, 230
Growth and income stock funds, 6, 16, 17, 19, 31, 38–41, 63, 72–73
Growth stock funds, 6, 16, 17, 19, 31, 37, 63
Gunn, John A., 201–203

Hague, John L., 83
The Handbook for No-Load Fund Investing (Jacobs), 25
Handicaps, of funds, 137–141
Harbor Bond, 64, 81–82, 103
Harbor Capital Advisors, 82, 108
Harbor International, 61, 90, 102, 140, 159, 206
Harris Associates, 37, 75, 257
Harvard University, 27, 191, 233
Hayes, Helen Young, 41
Heartland Advisors, 69
Heartland Value, 63, 69
Heine Associates, 38
Heine Securities, 35
Herro, David G., 75
Hidden load, 138
Higgins, Edward M., 24, 85, 125, 130, 151, 154, 164, 168
Higgins Associates, 24
High front-end load, 138
Hoffman, Robert T., 40

Hoisington, Van, 230
Holowesko, Mark G., 76, 87
Horn, Geraldine, 95
Horseman, John R., 44, 101, 102
Hotchkis and Wiley, 31, 43
Hotchkis and Wiley International, 42–43
Hulbert, Mark, 172
Humphries, Henrietta, 24 25, 85, 89, 112, 135, 150
Hunter College, 26

Ibbotson Associates, 4
Income Fund of America, 62
Income stock funds, 52–53, 63, 78–79
Index funds, 177–179
Individual Asset Planning, 25
Individual Investor, 26
Individual retirement account; *See* IRA
Individual securities, and funds, 167–168
Intel Corporation, 203
International bond funds, 6
International/Global bond funds, 18, 19, 32
International/Global bond stock funds, 64
International/Global bond stock futures, 83– 84
International/Global stock funds, 6, 16, 18, 19, 31, 41 45, 63, 73–74
Invesco Balanced, 32, 51–52, 78
Invesco Funds Group, 49, 51, 108
Invesco High Yield Bond, 62
Invesco Intermediate, 62
Invesco Strategic Health Sciences, 30, 32, 49
Investing for a Lifetime (Merriman), 25
Investment Company Institute, 3, 4, 24
Investors, versus traders, 119–122
Investor's Business Daily, 127
Investors Research, 34
IRA, 3, 18

Jacobs, Sheldon, 25, 125, 129, 130, 134, 138, 139, 144, 148, 149, 150, 155, 159, 161, 162, 168
Janus Capital, 41, 70
Janus Flexible Income, 62
Janus Fund, 30, 63, 70–71, 102, 108, 110, 149, 170, 213–218
Janus Overseas, 11, 29, 31
Janus 20, 102, 149, 219–222
Janus Worldwide, 31, 41–42

Kaplan, Paul D., 56

Kaufmann, 30, 62, 65
Kaye, Steven, 39
Kelly, Paul, 51
Ketterer, Sarah H., 43
Keys to Investing in Mutual Funds (Boroson), 23
Keystone, 111, 112, 113
Kigner, Jeffrey A., 47
King, Richard H., 42
Koch, Jeffrey A., 55
Kolluri, Ram, 25, 86, 89, 120–121, 125, 151, 173
Kurt Brouwer's Guide to Mutual Funds, 24

Lafayette College, 223
Laporte, John H., 70
Lehigh University, 241
Lehman Brothers Corporate/Government Bond Index, 17, 18
Lewis, Brad, 102
Lexington Management, 73
Lexington Worldwide Emerging Markets, 63, 73–74, 89–90
Liberty Media, 257
Lindner, 17, 62, 85, 112, 134
Lindner Dividend, 11, 29, 32, 52–53, 85, 90, 149
Lindner Growth, 122, 149
Lipper, Michael, 227
Litman, Craig, 25, 85, 89, 126, 130, 140, 144, 149, 150, 151, 162, 163, 167, 173
Litman/Gregory & Company, 25
Livermore, Jesse, 218
Loaded Questions on No-Load Funds (Berry), 23
Loomis-Sayles, 79, 187–190
Loomis-Sayles Bond, 63, 79–80
Lurito, Stephen J., 67
Lutts, 167
Lynch, Peter, 143, 149, 159, 196, 218, 222, 231

MacKinnon, Ian A., 58 59, 83, 223–231
Manager, performance, 157–160
Market-timers, 120–122
  typology of, 169–174
Market-timing
  arguments against, 172
  signals, 171
Market-Timing with No-Load Mutual Funds, 25
Markman, Robert, 25, 85, 89, 134, 139, 155

INDEX

Markman Capital Management, 25
Markman Multifunds, 25
Marsico, Thomas F., 102, 215, 219–222
Mathers, 90, 102
McCall, James, 93
McEvoy, Earl E., 53, 81
Meeder, Robert S., Jr., 86
Merger, 86, 87 88, 89, 102
Merrill Lynch, 25, 162
Merriman, Paul, 25, 86, 89, 120, 125, 135, 151, 155, 160, 163, 164, 173
Merriman Leveraged Growth, 89, 92–93
Merriman/Notaro, 92
Microsoft Corporation, 197, 203
Millard, Kathleen T., 40
Minnesota Mutual, 24
Mobius, Mark, 101, 102
Modern Investing in No-Load Funds (Pope), 26
Momentum-follower, 139
Monetta, 30, 90, 258
The Money Game (Smith), 218
Monrad, Ernest E., 54, 102
Montgomery, 112
Montgomery Small Cap, 62
Montgomery Value + Growth, 104–105
Morgan Stanley, 108, 109, 115–116
Morningstar, 206
Morningstar, Inc., 5, 20, 25, 124, 128, 219, 233
Morningstar Mutual Funds, 26
Morris, Charles A., 48, 211
Moses, Cedd, 91
MPL Communications, 26
Municipal bond funds, 6, 32
Municipal bond stock funds, 64, 82–83
Municipal fixed-income funds, 19
Municipal funds, 18
Murray, Jack, 101
Mussey, John M., 74, 102
Mutual Discovery, 11, 29, 31, 85
Mutual Fund Investing, 26
Mutual Funds Timing and Tactics and Strategies (Boroson), 23
Mutual Securities, 12
Mutual Series funds, 85, 108, 235–240
Mutual Shares, 122, 134
Mutual Shares/Beacon, 11, 29, 30, 31, 38

Nasgovitz, William J., 69
Neffs, John, 226, 231
Neuberger & Berman, 108, 109–110

Neuberger & Berman Guardian, 85, 90
Newell, Roger D., 47
Newport Fund Management, 74
Nicholas, Albert O., 102
Nicholas Limited, 62
No-Load Fund Analyst, 25
The No-Load Fund Investor (Jacobs), 25
NoLoad Fund*X, 23
No-Load Mutual Fund Guide (Donoghue), 24
No-Load Mutual Funds (Droms and Heerwagen), 24
Northeast Investors Trust, 11, 29, 32, 54, 90, 102
Northeast Investors Trustees, 54
Northwestern University, 251

Oakmark, 11, 29, 31, 37, 108, 109, 257–258
Oakmark International, 63, 74–75, 257–258
Ognar, Ronald C., 96
Oklahoma, University of, 235
One Up on Wall Street (Lynch), 218, 222
Open-end investment companies, versus closed-ends, 123–126
Oppenheimer Growth and Income, 102
Oracle, 203
Owens, Edward P., 47
Owens-Illinois, 109

Pacific Horizon High-Yield Bond, 80
Pacific Investment Management Company; *See* PIMCO
Paine Weber, 112
PBHG, 102, 108, 181–185
PBHG Emerging Growth, 157, 181–182
PBHG Growth, 11, 29, 31, 33, 181–185
PBHG Select Equity, 89, 93
Penn State, 223
Pennsylvania Mutual, 85, 151
Performance
    comparing, 129–131
    consistency of, 128–131
Performance reasons, of funds, 153–156
Perkins Opportunity, 61
Petersen, Stephen R., 77
Phillips, Don, 25, 86, 89, 120–121, 124, 126, 129, 131, 139, 140, 144–145, 151, 155, 159, 163, 168, 173
Pieralini, Fabrizio, 98
Pilgrim, Gary L., 33, 93, 102, 112, 181–185
Pilgrim Baxter & Associates, 33, 93

PIMCO, 83, 145, 205–206, 230
PIMCO Foreign Institutional, 64, 83–84
PIMCO Low Duration, 90
Pioneer Fund, 190
Pope, Alan, 13, 26, 85, 122, 124, 126, 131, 134, 139, 150, 168
Portfolio, assembling, 161–165
Portfolio managers
    interviews with, 175–258
    most admired, 101–105
Posner, Brian S., 46, 251–255
Price, Michael F., 35, 38, 85, 101–103, 102, 157, 235–240
Putnam, 108, 109, 116

R. Meeder & Associates, 86
RCM Global Technologies Fund, 89, 93–94
The Record, 23
Reminiscences of a Stock Operator (Livermore), 218
Risk-adjusted rating, for funds, 128
Robertson Stephens Contrarian, 89, 94
Robertson Stephens Investment Management, 94, 104, 108, 109
Robertson Stephens Emerging Growth, 15, 140
Robertson Stephens Investment Management, 15
Rogers, Brian C., 45, 102, 191–194
Royal Dutch Petroleum, 239
Ruane, William, 102
Rukeyser, Louis, 25
Ryan, Jack, 241–249
Ryback, Eric E., 52
Ryback Management, 52

Saler, Richard T., 73
Sales charge, deferred, 138
Sams, William, 102, 145
Sanborn, Robert J., 37, 101–102, 257–258
San Francisco, University of, 24
Santella, Gloria J., 66
Sarnell, Melody P., 47
Sauter, George U., 40
Savage, Stephen, 26, 85, 130, 134, 160
Schabacker, Jay, 26, 85, 89, 109, 125, 131, 138, 139, 145, 151, 165, 167
Schabacker Investment Management, 26
Schooner, 89, 94–95
Schroer, John R., 49

Schwab 1000, 89
Scudder, 108, 111
Scudder Emerging Markets Income, 64, 84
Scudder Equity-Income Fund, 40
Scudder Growth and Income, 30, 31, 40–41
Scudder Income, 62
Scudder International Bond, 30
Scudder Stevens & Clark, 40, 84
Securities and Exchange Commission (SEC), 23
Security Income Fund High-Yield, 80
Selected American, 233
Sequoia, 61, 102, 237
Sheldon Jacob's Guide to Successful No-Load Fund Investing (Jacob), 25
Size, as a fund handicap, 143–145
Skala, Martin, 26, 86, 89, 109, 116, 121, 125, 139, 148, 151, 154, 160, 164, 168
Small company stock funds, 6, 16, 17, 19, 31, 35–36, 63, 67–72
Smith, Adam, 218
Smith, Bonnie L., 87, 102
Smith, Morris, 149
Societe Generale Asset Management, 75
SoGen International, 30, 63, 75–76
Soros, George, 217
Spare, Anthony E., 47
Specialty stock funds, 6, 16, 18, 19, 47–49, 63, 77–78
Stability, 128–131
Standard & Poor's 500, 129, 162, 171, 172, 199
Standard & Poor's 500 Stock Index, 17, 18, 39
Stanford University, 23, 24, 195
Stansky, Robert E., 103
State Teachers Retirement System of Ohio, 257
Steadman, Charles, 111, 112, 115
Stein, John Picard, 27, 85, 89, 111, 125, 134, 138, 139, 140, 148, 159, 162, 163, 167
Stein No-Load Mutual Fund Service, 27
Stein Roe, 112
Stein Roe Capital Opportunities, 62, 65–66
Stein Roe & Farnham, 66, 233
Stephens, Paul H., 94
Stock funds, 17–19, 31–32, 33–53, 62–84
    aggressive growth, 33–35, 62, 64–67
    balanced, 49–52, 63, 78
    classification of, 6

INDEX

Stock funds—*continued*
    corporate bond, 63 64, 79–81
    equity income, 45–47, 63, 77
    government bonds, 64, 81–82
    growth, 37, 63
    growth and income, 38 41, 63, 72–73
    income, 52–53, 63, 78–79
    international/global, 41–45, 63, 64, 73–74
    municipal bond, 64, 82–83
    small company, 35–36, 63, 67–72
    specialty, 47–49, 63, 77–78
Stock futures, international/global, 83–84
Stock mutual funds, classifications of, 16
Stowers, James E. III, 35, 210
Strategy, 139
    lack of, 138
Strong, 108
Strong Capital Management, 55, 71, 96
Strong Corporate Bond, 32, 54–55
Strong Funds Distributors, 56
Strong Government, 30
Strong Government Securities, 11, 29, 32, 55–56
Strong Growth, 89, 96
Strong Opportunity, 63, 71
Strong Total Return, 63, 78
Student Loan Marketing Association, 55
Successful Investing in No-Load Funds (Pope), 26
Sylvia Porter's Personal Finance Magazine, 23

T. Rowe Price Associates, 12, 36, 45, 48, 70, 80, 108, 109, 191–194, 195–200, 211–212, 223
T. Rowe Price Capital Appreciation, 90
T. Rowe Price Equity-Income, 11, 29, 30, 31, 45, 85, 102
T. Rowe Price High Yield, 64, 80–81
T. Rowe Price International, 30, 32
T. Rowe Price International Bond, 11, 29, 30
T. Rowe Price International Stock, 31, 43
T. Rowe Price Investment Services, 43, 57, 79
T. Rowe Price New Asia, 62
T. Rowe Price New Horizons, 63, 69–70
T. Rowe Price New Income, 62
T. Rowe Price Science & Technology, 32, 48 49, 211–212
T. Rowe Price Small Cap Value, 31, 36–37, 195

T. Rowe Price Spectrum Income, 63, 78–79
Take Charge! A Step-by-Step Guide to Managing Your Money (Humphries), 25
Tank, Bradley C., 56
Templeton, John, 108, 109, 237
Templeton Developing Markets, 102
Templeton Foreign, 63, 76
Templeton Galbraith & Hansberger, 76, 86
Templeton Growth, 86
Texas, University of, 25–26
Texas Christian University, 207
Thayer, Peter, 102
Thieme, Heiko, 102
Third Avenue Value, 89–90, 96–97, 102
Thomas, Lee R., 83
Thorndike, Benjamin W., 40
Tillinghast, Joel C., 68
Time periods, stressing of, 133–135
Total returns, 128–131
    annualized, 20
Traders, versus investors, 119–122
Trust Company of the West, 213
Tufts/New England Medical Center, 24
Tulsa, University of, 181
Turnover ratio, 20
Twentieth Century, 109, 139
Twentieth Century Balanced, 62
Twentieth Century Giftrust, 61, 207–210
Twentieth Century Growth, 165
Twentieth Century Select, 209
Twentieth Century Ultra, 31, 34–35, 128, 130, 165
Twentieth Century Vista, 210

UCLA, 206
United Services, 108
United Services Bonnel Growth, 89, 97
United States Treasury bills, 4
U.S. Global Investors, Inc., 97
USAA Mutual Income, 62
USA Today, 25
Utah, University of, 233
Utsch, Hans, 65

Valley Forge Fund, 128
Value Line, 26
Value Line Income, 62
Value Line Leveraged Growth, 62
Value Line Mutual Fund Survey, 128

The Value Line Mutual Fund Survey (Savage), 26
van der Eb, Henry, Jr., 102
Van Dyke, Peter, 79
Vanguard Asset Allocation, 63, 78
Vanguard Equity-Income, 30, 32, 46–47
Vanguard Fixed-Income GNMA, 56–57
Vanguard Fixed-Income Group, 82
Vanguard GNMA, 30, 32
Vanguard Group, 12, 17, 19, 47, 56, 58, 59, 108, 109, 145, 177–179, 223–231, 258
Vanguard High Yield Bond, 62
Vanguard Index 500, 31, 39–40, 85
Vanguard Insured Long-Term, 32
Vanguard Limited-Term Municipal, 64
Vanguard Long-Term Corporate, 64, 81
Vanguard Municipal Insured Long-Term, 58–59
Vanguard Municipal Intermediate, 11, 29, 30, 32, 58
Vanguard Municipal Limited-Term, 82–83
Vanguard Muni High Yield, 62
Vanguard's Core Management Group, 39
Vanguard Specialized Health Care, 32, 47–48
Vanguard STAR, 229–230
Vanguard U.S. Growth Fund, 179
Vanguard/Wellesley Income, 30, 32, 53, 241–249
Vanguard/Wellington, 30, 32, 50–51, 78, 85
Vanguard/Windsor, 61, 226
Vanguard/Windsor, II, 62, 86, 88
Van Wagoner fund, 61
Vinik, Jeffrey, 101–103, 149
Virginia, University of, 241
Volatility, 127–131, 138, 139
von Metzsch, Ernst H., 51
Vontobel Europacific, 89, 98
Vontobel USA, 98

Wade, Martin G., 43
Wallace, John, 102
Wall Street Journal, 237
"Wall Street Week," 25, 140
Wal-Mart, 197, 242
Wanger, Ralph, 102, 257
Warburg Pincus Counsellors, 42, 67, 98
Warburg Pincus Emerging Growth, 62, 66–67
Warburg Pincus International Equity, 31
Warburg Pincus International Equity-Common Shares, 42
Warburg Pincus Japan OTC, 89, 98–99
Washington Post, 212
W.E. Donoghue & Co., 24
Weber, Ken, 27, 85, 89, 112, 121–122, 125, 130, 139, 149, 151, 158, 161
Weber Asset Management, 27
Weber's Fund Advisor, 27
Weiss, Richard T., 71
Wellington Advisors, 17
Wellington Management Company, 47, 51, 53, 81, 241
Westchester Capital Management, 87
Western Union Corporation, 24
The Wharton School, 213
Whitman, Martin J., 97, 102
Wiesenberger Investment Companies Service, 26
Windsor Fund, 179
Worth Magazine, 26

Yacktman, Donald A., 63, 72, 85, 102, 233–234
Yacktman Asset Management, 72, 86
Yacktman Fund's, 233–234
Yale University, 195

Ziegler, Carlene Murphy, 67, 102
Zweig, Martin, 172